COLLINS
WORDPOWER

Punctuation
Graham King

HarperCollins*Publishers*

HarperCollins*Publishers*
Westerhill Road, Bishopbriggs, Glasgow G64 2QT

First published 2000

Reprint 10 9 8 7 6 5 4 3 2 1

© 2000 Estate of Graham King

Cartoons by Hunt Emerson

ISBN 0 00 472373 2

A catalogue record for this book is available from the British Library

Typeset by Davidson Pre-Press Graphics Ltd, Glasgow G3

Printed and bound in Great Britain by
Omnia Books Ltd, Glasgow G64

Contents

Graham King (1930-1999)

Graham King was born in Adelaide on October 16, 1930.
He trained as a cartographer and draughtsman before joining
Rupert Murdoch's burgeoning media empire in the 1960s, where
he became one of Murdoch's leading marketing figures during the
hard-fought Australian newspaper circulation wars of that decade.
Graham King moved to London in 1969, where his marketing
strategy transformed the *Sun* newspaper into the United
Kingdom's bestselling tabloid; subsequently, after 1986, he
successfully promoted the reconstruction of *The Sunday Times* as
a large multi-section newspaper.

A poet, watercolourist, landscape gardener and book
collector, Graham King also wrote a biography of Zola, *Garden of
Zola* (1978) and several thrillers such as *Killtest* (1978). Other
works include the novel *The Pandora Valley* (1973), a semi-
autobiographical account of the hardships endured by the
Australian unemployed and their families set in the 1930s.

In the early 1990s, inspired by the unreadability and
impracticality of many of the guides to English usage in
bookshops, Graham King developed the concept of a series of
reference guides called The One-Hour Wordpower series:

accessible, friendly guides designed to guide the reader through the maze of English usage. He later expanded and revised the texts to create an innovative series of English usage guides that would break new ground in their accessibility and usefulness. The new range of reference books became the Collins Wordpower series (see page 185), the first four titles being published in March 2000, the second four in May 2000. Graham King died in May 1999, shortly after completing the Collins Wordpower series.

> **PUNCTUATION.** *n.* [*punctum,* Latin]. **1. The use of symbols not belonging to the alphabet to indicate intonation and meaning not otherwise conveyed in the written language. 2. The symbols used for this purpose.**

Introduction

Punctuation makes possible the clear presentation of the written language.

Or, as one British newspaper advises its writers, punctuation is 'a courtesy designed to help readers to understand a story without stumbling'. It is the nuts and bolts of the language.

There is a strong view that punctuation is more important than spelling. Dr Temple, a former Archbishop of York, thought so. 'Now spelling is one of the decencies of life, like the proper use of knives and forks,' he wrote in 1938. But, 'if you are getting your commas, semicolons and full stops wrong, it means that you are not getting your thoughts right, and your mind is muddled.'

Despite the importance of punctuation in effective communication, there seems today to be a woeful indifference to and ignorance about using even its simplest forms.

Or can it be fear? If so, then punctuation's scary image is undeserved, as you'll soon discover in this book. Although designed as an all-inclusive, authoritative reference work it will guarantee to take the perils out of punctuation quickly, efficiently and – yes – entertainingly.

Punctuation – What's the Point?

Those dots, strokes and squiggles may appear physically insignificant on a page of print and evanescent in our speech, but without them all would be chaos. Not knowing how to use them properly can result in even greater chaos. If you were to say to someone:

I hate habitual liars; like you, I find them detestable.

that person would very likely agree. But imagine the reaction should you tinker slightly with the punctuation:

I hate habitual liars like you; I find them detestable.

You're looking at a system that's some 2,500 years old. The Greeks came up with the germ of the idea but it took until the Middle Ages for our present system to emerge and a further 500 years for it to acquire its final polish.

Perhaps encouraged by a full complement of marks, writing became very elaborate. Its more skilled practitioners – say, Jane Austen and Charles Dickens – loved to punctuate, and their stately prose is speckled with all manner of stops and symbols. Sentences held together by a score or more commas, semi-colons, brackets, dashes and other marks are commonplace.

Nowadays sentences, no doubt influenced by the brevity of newspaper style, are shorter, and the need for the complicated division of long sentences has all but disappeared. Commas are freely dropped where the meaning remains unaffected. Stops after abbreviations are disappearing in a general quest for typographic tidiness. Today the majority of the English-speaking population probably goes through life without ever using, on paper, any punctuation marks other than the comma, dash and full stop.

Don't, however, be led astray by this easy-going tolerance. While parsimony in punctuation may be adequate for the majority, it will be of little use to you if you wish to improve your communication skills. The role of punctuation in writing good English cannot be underestimated.

Understanding Punctuation

Is there a trick secret to understanding punctuation?

No, but it does help if you know something about its past. Two or three centuries ago most punctuation took its cues from speech. This was an age when the predominant practice of reading aloud, with its breath pauses and dramatic stresses, was translated into written punctuation – rhetorical punctuation.

A hundred years on, with increased literacy, the spoken word gave way to the written. The stress now was on meaning rather than dramatic effect, and rhetorical (or oratorical) punctuation bowed to a more logical system.

Today we think we have a practical blend of both: a system capable of conveying feelings, force, urgency, tension, rhythm and passion while never abandoning its duty to consistency and clarity of meaning.

Here's an example of how a sentence might have been written, say, 150 years ago, compared with the same sentence today. The first reflects the natural pauses of speech: it is meant to be *heard* rather than read. The second is directed primarily to the eye and the mind, rather than to the ear.

3

Everyone in the cast knew, that Pamela would wish to be the
star performer, and once having achieved that status would
look down on the rest.

Everyone in the cast knew that Pamela would wish to be the
star performer and, once having achieved that status, would
look down on the rest.

With the invention and growth of printing, the need for
punctuation was inevitable, and publishers have played a vital part
in its development. With punctuation, a page of type became more
inviting and easier to read, and self-interested publishers ensured
that the system was refined and permanent. More than any other
group, publishers of newspapers, magazines and books are our
punctuation police, the custodians of the language. But publishers
are also human and thus prone to sloppiness and error, as the
many examples of punctuation bloopers and barbarisms in this
book will attest.

None of us should ever take punctuation for granted!

Collins Wordpower Makes Punctuation Easy

Anyone who reads and writes needs to possess a good
working knowledge of English grammar, and that includes
punctuation. Any piece of writing will fall apart without the nuts
and bolts of punctuation.

It's an irony that although the wonderful communicating
tool known as English is the second most widely used language in
the world today, it is also probably the most abused and misused.
During the last few decades millions of British schoolchildren were

denied any formal instruction in important aspects of grammar and punctuation.

Now, as adults, many lack confidence when they come to put pen to paper or finger to keyboard. Fortunately there are signs that near-illiteracy is no longer the fashion, and the urge to improve writing skills (judging from the sales of dictionaries and language books) is growing at a phenomenal rate.

This book is intended for all those people for whom punctuation is a plague of spots and dots and marks. The role of punctuation in writing good English is demonstrated step by logical, practical step. Hundreds of examples help explain in seconds what hours of former teaching – or the lack of it – never managed to impart.

And take heart! Somerset Maugham couldn't handle commas. Jane Austen got her quotation marks in a twist. George Orwell feared semicolons so much he wrote a novel without any at all. The competition isn't so awesome after all.

Collins Wordpower: Punctuation is an easy-going refresher course that banishes forever hassles with hyphens, catastrophes with apostrophes, confusion with commas. After an hour or two with this book the perils of punctuation should exist no more.

Punctuation for the Birds

The following passage employs all the punctuation marks used in writing English. They are, in order of appearance: capital letter, italic and bold emphasis, asterisk, semicolon, comma, parenthesis, colon, full stop, double quotation marks, contraction apostrophe, question mark, exclamation mark, underline, dash, hyphens, possessive apostrophe, square brackets, stroke, single quotation marks, and three-dot ellipsis.

The habits of the ***Rook**** are very interesting and easily watched; hours can be wasted in early spring observing them as, cawing incessantly, they gather in their rookery to build or repair their large nests in the topmost branches, causing a rain of twigs and sticks to fall on the garden below (and not only on the garden: my brother was almost knocked out after being hit by a branch of Scots pine. "What's that?" he cried out, obviously dazed. "A tree's fallen on me!") and which are never retrieved. Worse, of course, is to be struck by a <u>dead</u> rook – the weak and ne'er-do-wells are executed and expelled from their nests – and anyone blitzed by a half-kilo chunk of solid rook's meat can say with some feeling [the editor concurs, having had just such an experience/calamity] that walking under a rookery is definitely 'for the birds' . . .

* And this is a footnote.

A Victorian Schoolmistress's 10 Golden Rules of Punctuation

Sentences begin with a *Capital letter*,
So as to make your writing better.

Use a *full stop* to mark the end.
It closes every sentence penned.

The *comma* is for short pauses and breaks,
And also for lists the writer makes.

Dashes – like these – are for thoughts by the way.
They give extra information (so do *brackets* we may say).

These two dots are *colons*: they pause to compare.
They also do this: list, explain, and prepare.

The *semicolon* makes a break; followed by a clause.
It does the job of words that link; it's also a short pause.

An *apostrophe* shows the owner of anyone's things,
And it's also useful for shortenings.

I'm so glad! He's so mad! We're having such a lark!
To show strong feelings use an *exclamation mark!*

A *question mark* follows What? When? Where? Why?
  and How?
Do you? Can I? Shall we? Give us your answer now!

"Quotation marks" enclose what is said,
Which is why they're sometimes called "speech marks"
  instead.

Units of Space

Sentences and Paragraphs

Space is a basic form of punctuation. It separates words, sentences, paragraphs and larger units such as chapters.

Historically, in mediaeval manuscripts and early books, sentences were separated by a variety of decorative devices. But with the advent of printing this labour-intensive practice was dropped in favour of plain spaces: small spaces between words, larger spaces between sentences, and fresh lines – sometimes indented – for paragraphs, as in this book.

Early capital letters were typically highly ornamented to draw attention to the start of a sentence. Today, although we have dropped the ornamentation, the capital still conventionally serves as a marker for the beginning of sentences and proper names and is also used for several other functions.

The sentence is about the most common of all grammatical units. We speak in sentences. The most untutored letter-writers among us will use them while ignoring every other form of punctuation. So the sentence seems to be a good place to begin a discussion about punctuation.

The Unique Nature of the Sentence

So, what *is* a sentence? The *Oxford English Dictionary's* famous definition was: 'Such portion of a composition or utterance as extends from one full stop to another.' More recently (1998) the *Collins English Dictionary* described the sentence as 'a sequence of words capable of standing alone to make an assertion, ask a question, or give a command, usually consisting of a subject and a predicate containing a finite verb.' And there are dozens more stabs by eminent grammarians at defining what a sentence is and is not, which is surprising as the unit has been around for some 1,500 years.

What the grammarians seem to miss is the sentence's quality of uniqueness. The American philologist Professor Stephen Pinker delights in pointing this out.

> 'Go into the Library of Congress,' he suggests, 'and pick a sentence at random from any volume, and chances are you would fail to find an exact repetition no matter how long you continued to search. Estimates of the number of sentences that an ordinary person is capable of producing are breathtaking . . . Let's assume that a person is capable of producing sentences up to twenty words long. Therefore the number of sentences that a speaker can deal with in principle is at least a hundred million trillion (100,000,000,000,000,000,000).'

If that statistic puts you into a spin, at least the functions of the sentence are quite straightforward:

- To make statements.

- To ask questions.

- To request action.

- To express feelings.

It's also reasonable to say that a sentence should express a single idea, and that it should be complete in thought and construction. Like this:

> *The rare great crested newt was once called the great warty newt.*

The sentence can be quite elastic, and punctuation allows us to expand this useful unit:

> *The rare great crested newt, which is native to Britain and rarely exceeds fifteen centimetres in length, was once called the great warty newt.*

You'll notice how the cunning commas have enabled us to double the length of the sentence without sacrificing any of its original clarity.

Sentences can also shrink, often alarmingly:

> *'Don't!'*

That single word, providing it is given meaning by other words and thoughts surrounding it, is a sentence, or more accurately, a sentence fragment. Here it is, now in a context that provides its relevance and meaning:

> *I went over to the door and tried to open it.*
> *'Don't!'*
> *I spun around, searching for the owner of the angry voice.*
> *In the darkness, a face appeared . . .*

You can see that not only the surrounding words, but also a range of spaces and punctuation marks, help to give that single word the meaning intended. Here is another example, the opening of Charles Dickens's novel *Bleak House*:

*London. Michaelmas Term lately over, and the Lord
Chancellor sitting in Lincoln's Inn Hall. Implacable
November weather. As much mud in the streets, as if the
waters had but newly retired from the face of the earth, and
it would not be wonderful to meet a Megalosaurus, forty feet
long or so, waddling like an elephantine lizard up Holborn
Hill. Smoke lowering down from chimney-pots, making a
soft black drizzle, with flakes of soot in it as big as full-grown
snow-flakes – gone into mourning, one might imagine,
for the death of the sun. Dogs, undistinguishable in mire.
Horses, scarcely better; splashed to their very blinkers.*

13

> *Foot passengers, jostling one another's umbrellas, in a*
> *general infection of ill-temper, and losing their foot-hold at*
> *street-corners, where tens of thousands of other foot*
> *passengers have been slipping and sliding since the day broke*
> *(if this day ever broke), adding new deposits to the crust upon*
> *crust of mud, sticking at those points tenaciously to the*
> *pavement, and accumulating at compound interest.*

The first three sentences in this passage are not grammatical sentences at all, and most grammarians would choke over several of the others, too. But it is such a vivid evocation of a miserable rainy November day in Victorian London that few would dare to challenge the novelist's masterly manipulation of the language. Or argue too much about 'proper' sentences. At least they are punctuated correctly; they all start with a capital letter and finish with a full stop.

How Long is a Sentence?

A question that crops up with astonishing regularity is, 'How long should a sentence be?' The usual answer is, neither too long nor too short. A sensible approach is to regard short sentences as more easily understood than long, complicated ones, but an endless succession of staccato sentences can be irritating to the reader. It really comes down to judgment. Careful writers will 'hear' their work as they proceed; that way the sentences will form themselves into a logical, interesting, economical and, with luck, elegant flow of thought.

Here's a piece of prose that's more a form of mental torture than sentence:

*A person shall be treated as suffering from physical
disablement such that he is either unable to walk or virtually
unable to do so if he is not unable or virtually unable to walk
with a prosthesis or an artificial aid which he habitually
wears or uses or if he would not be unable or virtually unable
to walk if he habitually wore or used a prosthesis or an
artificial aid which is suitable in his case.*

That is a grammatical sentence written by someone
expecting it to be understood, but it defies understanding.
Yet what it is trying to say is something very simple and which
can be unambiguously expressed in our ideal sentence, *'complete in
thought and construction'*:

*Persons are regarded as physically disabled if they always
need an artificial aid to walk.*

As you can see, sentences can be grammatical without
making any sense. The linguist Noam Chomsky proved this by
forming a chain of words that bore the least logical relationship
with each other: *Colourless green ideas sleep furiously*. The words make
no sense but it is a well-formed sentence complete with verb.

The Paragraph

The most quoted definition of a paragraph is that of Sir
Ernest Gowers, who wrote in *The Complete Plain Words* that it is 'a
unit of thought, not of length . . . homogeneous in subject matter
and sequential in treatment of it.' *The Times*, in advising its
journalists, adds: 'Rarely should a paragraph in *The Times* be of
only one sentence, least of all a short one, unless special emphasis

is needed. Long paragraphs are tedious but short ones are jerky and can be equally hard to follow. The best advice is to remember Gowers and ask, before pressing the paragraph key, "Have I finished that thought?".'

All very well, but of all the units of punctuation the paragraph is the least precise and the most resistant to rules. Sometimes they are indented, sometimes not. Quite often, the first paragraph under a heading is not indented, although all subsequent paragraphs are. Browse through a handful of books and you'll note that paragraphs can consist of a single line or a single word; you'll also see leviathan examples which take up a page or more.

Here are some practical pointers. Think of the end of a paragraph as a sort of breathing space for both writer and listener. The writer needs to gather his thoughts afresh, and the reader needs a momentary rest from concentration. In writing, a new paragraph marks a break or change in the flow of thought, which is as good a reason as any to begin on a fresh line.

Capitalisation

Capital letters are an important form of punctuation in that they help to guide the eye and mind through a text. Try this:

> *mi5 is the branch of the british intelligence organisation responsible for internal security and counter-espionage in the united kingdom. mi6 is the branch responsible for international espionage. the us has its fbi, south africa has its boss, israel its mossad and the republic of ireland its g2. spies love abbreviations. Then, in britain there's mi1, mi8, mi9 and, ultimately, wx, the butlins of the spy world.*

That's a paragraph shorn of capital letters. It's readable, with some effort, but how much easier would the eye glide through it were the beginnings of sentences and names guide-posted with capital letters – not to mention abbreviations!

Using capitals to flag the start of sentences is clear enough but confusion surrounds the capitalising of certain nouns and names. Try this Capital Quiz:

Capital Quiz

Of this dozen nouns and names, half are incorrect. Which ones?
the Army, Spring and Autumn, bulldog, Great Dane, union jack, Vincent Van Gogh, jacuzzi, french fries, Renaissance, Venus, new testament, down under.

*[**Answers:** the army, spring and autumn, Union Jack, Vincent van Gogh, Jacuzzi, New Testament, Down Under. The others are correct.]*

Some capitalisations are logical but many are not. Some are consistent throughout the language while others are arbitrary, differing from country to country and even from one publisher or newspaper to another. Here, as a guideline, are the generally accepted capitalisations for a range of fairly common nouns and names.

A Guide to Capitalisation

Sentences   Begin every sentence with a capital letter.

First Person   Always capitalised: *I said I was going out.*

Pronoun	Capitals do not follow commas, semicolons or colons except where the following word is a name or proper noun.
Aircraft	*Concorde, Boeing 747, Fokker*, etc.
Armed Forces	*British Army, Italian Navy, Brazilian Air Force*, but *army, navy, air force. The Royal Marines*, but *marine*. Ranks are capitalised: *Sergeant, Admiral, Lieutenant*, etc.
The Calendar	*Monday, March, Good Friday, the Millennium Dome* but *the new millennium*.
Compass Points	*north-west, south-south-west*, but *mysterious East, deep South*, frozen *North*.
Days	*Christmas Day, Derby Day, New Year's Day*, etc, but *happy new year*.
The Deity	*God, Father, Holy Ghost, Holy Spirit, Almighty, Jehovah, Supreme Being, Jesus Christ, Son of Man, Holy Trinity, Redeemer, Saviour, He, Him, Thee, Thou; Virgin Mary, the Virgin, Madonna, the Holy Mother, Our Lady; Allah, Buddha, Muhammad,* the *Prophet*, etc; *Holy Bible, New Testament, Book of Common Prayer, Ten Commandments*; all names from the Bible. *Hades*, but *hell; heaven* but *Heaven* when referring to the Deity.
Diplomatic	*Nicaraguan embassy* (*embassy* is usually lower case)

18

Dog Breeds	*Capitalised: Afghan hound, Airedale terrier, Basenji, Great Dane, Kerry blue, Labrador, Newfoundland, Pomeranian, Samoyed, Schnauzer, Cairns terrier, Scotch terrier.* *Lower case: basset hound, bulldog, bull terrier, cocker spaniel, golden retriever, lurcher, pug, poodle, rottweiler.* Check a good dictionary for other breeds.
Exclamations	*Oh! Ahrrgh! Wow!*
Flora and Fauna	*Arab horse, Shetland pony, Montague's harrier,* but *hen harrier* (caps where proper name is involved). Plants are lower case but with scientific names, orders, classes, families and genuses are capitalised; species and varieties are lc: *Agaricus bisporus.*
Geographical	*the West, the East, the Orient, Northern Hemisphere, Third World, British Commonwealth, the Gulf, the Midlands, the Levant, the Continent, the Tropics, the Left Bank,* etc, but *eastern counties, facing north, oriental life, tropical fruit, northern Britain, western fashions.*
Headlines	With cap and lc headlines, capitalise nouns, pronouns, verbs and words of four or more letters. Generally, capitalise *No, Not, Off, Out, So* and *Up* but not *a, and, as, at, but, by, for, if, in, of, on, the, to* – except when they begin headlines. Capitalise both parts of hyphenated compounds: *Sit-In, Cease-Fire, Post-War.*

Heavenly Bodies	*Mars, Venus, Ursa Major, Halley's Comet, Southern Cross, Milky Way*, etc.
History and Historical Names	*Cambrian Era, Middle Ages, Elizabethan, the Depression, Renaissance, Year of the Rat, Georgian, Victorian* etc.
Law and Lords	*Lord Chancellor, Black Rod, Master of the Rolls, Lord Privy Seal, Queen's Counsel.*
Local Government	*council*, but *Kent County Council, Enfield Borough Council, Lord Mayor of Manchester.*
Member of Parliament	*member of parliament*, but when abbreviated, *MP*.
Nations, Nationalities	*Venezuela, Alaska, Brits, Estonians, Sudanese; Arabic, Latin, Hellenic, Parisian. Indian ink, Indian file, Indian clubs* but *indian summer. French polish, French stick, French kiss, French letter* but *french window. Morocco* but *morocco bound. Chinese* but *chinaware; Turkish bath, Turkish delight.*
Personification	The family gods were *Hope* and *Charity*.
Political Parties, terms	*Tory, Conservative Party, Labour Party, Liberal Democrats, Communist Party* but *communist, communism; Thatcherism, Leninist, Luddites, Marxist, Gaullist* etc.
The Pope	*the Pope* but *popes; Pope Paul, Pope John* etc.
Proper Names	Names of people (*Tony Blair, Spice Girls*); places (*Europe, Sydney, Mt Everest*); titles (*Pride and Prejudice, Nine O'Clock News*);

epithets (*Iron Duke*, *Iron Lady*); nicknames (*'Tubby' Isaacs*, *'Leadfoot' Evans*).

Quotations   Capitalise the first word of complete quotations (*The boss asked him, 'Well, where's the money?'*), but not partial quotations, words or phrases.

Races   *Aztecs, Shawnees, Aboriginals, Asiatic.*

Religious Names   *the Church of England, the Roman Catholic Church* etc, but *church, synagogue, temple, cathedral. Rev Adam Black, Fr O'Brien, Sister Wendy, Mother Teresa, Archbishop of Canterbury; Catholics, Jew, Jewish, Semitic, anti-Semitism, Protestants*, etc.

Royalty   *The Queen, Duke of Edinburgh, Prince of Wales, Queen Mother, Princess Anne, the Crown.*

Our Rulers   *Her Majesty's Government, House of Commons, Prime Minister* (*PM* when abbreviated), *Secretary of State, Chancellor of the Exchequer.*

Satirised References   *In Crowd, Heavy Brigade, She Who Must Be Obeyed, Bright Young Things, Her Indoors.*

Scouts   *Scouts, Guides, Cubs.*

Seasons   *spring, summer, autumn, winter* (all lc).

Ships   *Cutty Sark, HMS Invincible, Titanic.*

Street Names   *road, avenue, crescent, square* etc, but *Highfield Road, Spring Avenue, Eagle Crescent, Sloane Square.*

Titles	*Sir Thomas More, Lord Asquith, Mr and Mrs, Dr*, etc.
Trade Marks, Names	*Hoover, Peugeot, Kentucky Fried Chicken, Gillette, Durex, Xerox, Aspro, Kodak, Persil, Jacuzzi* etc.

Van, Von etc When writing Dutch names, *van* is lower case when part of the full name (*Hans van Meegeren, Vincent van Gogh*) but capitalised when used only with the surname (*Van Gogh, Van Dyke*). One exception is former US president *Martin Van Buren*. The same applies to *den* (*Joop den Uyl, Mr Den Uyl*). With Germanic names, *von* is always lc. With *Da* and *D'* prefixes (*Mayor D'Amato, Louise d'Amato*) there is often inconsistency; such names require checking.

Wars *World War I, Boer War, Seven Years' War* etc.

Miscellany *Americanisation, anglicise, bologna sausage, braille, Central American, Caesarean section* (but *cesarean* in US), *Cheshire cheese, French dressing, Gothic architecture* (but *gothic novel*), *lyonnaise potatoes, madras cloth, melba toast, mid-Atlantic, Oxford Bags* (but *oxford shoe*), *plaster of paris, Pre-Raphaelite, the Post Office* (but *post office services*), *roman type, Russian roulette, Southerner, southern hemisphere, Spanish omelette* (*spanish* in US), *transatlantic, Trans-Siberian Railway, Union Jack.*

Pride and Prejudice *and Punctuation*

When Jane Austen's *Pride and Prejudice* was published
in 1813 our system of punctuation had developed to the
stage where few further changes would be made.
But one patch of inconsistency lingered: the practice
of not always treating question and exclamation marks
as doing the job of full stops:

*"And poor Mr Darcy! dear Lizzie, only consider what he must have
suffered. Such a disappointment! and with the knowledge of your
ill opinion too! and having to relate such a thing to his sister!
It is really too distressing, I am sure you must feel it so."
"What say you, Mary? for you are a lady of deep reflection,
I know, and read great books . . . "
"It is unaccountable! in every view it is unaccountable!"*

Today, of course, question marks and exclamation marks
are almost always followed by capitals.

Devices for
Separating and
Joining

Scree-e-e-eechh! The Full Stop.

Now we shrink from the paragraph to a minuscule dot: the full stop, stop, full point or period. Minuscule it may be but, like atoms and germs, it packs a potent power. The full stop is the most emphatic, abrupt and unambiguous of all the punctuation marks. Leave out a vital full stop and you're really in trouble:

> *KING CHARLES I PRAYED HALF AN HOUR AFTER HE WAS BEHEADED.*

The full stop is probably the most used mark, partly because we need it so much, and partly because virtually everyone knows how to use it. Unfortunately not everyone knows how to use it wisely.

"Punctuation," *The Times* advises its journalists, "is . . . not a fireworks display to show off your dashes and gaspers. Remember the first rule: the best punctuation is the full stop."

The full stop is used like a knife to cut off a sentence at the required length. The rule is *that* simple: where you place your stop is up to you, but as we saw in the chapter on the sentence it is generally at the point where a thought is complete. Master this principle and you can then move on to using full stops stylistically.

26

Here's a typical passage displaying a variety of punctuation marks; the full stop, though, is easily the most predominant:

> *With intense frustration, Giles grabbed the man, surprising him. 'No you don't!' he yelled hoarsely. The stranger recovered, fighting back. Fiercely. Savagely. Hard breathing. Curses. Grunts. The wincing thud of fists. An alarming stream of crimson from Giles's left eye. Pulses racing, they glared at one another, each daring the other to make a move. A car horn in the distance. Shouts.*

That's stylised prose and could be criticised for its overuse of sentence fragments rather than complete sentences. But here the heavy-handed application of the full stop is deliberate, for we can see what the writer is getting at – the brutal punch, punch, punch of a ferocious fist fight.

We can also see from that example just how important the full stop is, although there have been numerous attempts to do without it. One of the most famous examples is the Penelope chapter in James Joyce's novel *Ulysses*:

> ' . . . *a quarter after what an earthly hour I suppose they're just getting up in China now combing out their pigtails for the day well soon have the nuns ringing the angelus theyve nobody coming in to spoil their sleep except an odd priest or two for his night office the alarm clock next door* . . .

[until about a thousand words later]

> ' . . . *and first I put my arms around him yes and drew him down to me so he could feel my breasts all perfume yes and his heart was going like mad and yes I said yes I will Yes.*'

You did notice the full stop at the very end, didn't you? At least James Joyce decided to observe the rule that every sentence, however long, must end with a full stop or some other ending device.

Of course that's an extreme case, with Joyce chucking out all stops to achieve the effect of a stream of consciousness outpouring. At the other end of the scale is prose that goes full stop mad, such as this excerpt from Alain Arias-Misson's *Confessions*. The style was considered highly novel in the 1970s:

> *Fischer shot a glance at me. Listen, Fischer, I said, is there any way out of here? You are not an initiate, he said. Of course I addressed myself to him because I hoped there might be a model in his game. I watched the pieces under his eyes.*

*Ah yes, I said, I see. How curious, I thought, as I stood up,
that I hadn't realised it until now. I didn't know what move
to make next. The next move may be death, he said. I moved
my piece and walked out of the room. He was no longer
outside of the game. He was of course a free agent. I knew it
would be necessary to listen carefully, in this suspended
atmosphere. The master player had shown me a trick or two.
It was a matter of life and death.*

Again, the author is using punctuation for special effect,
in this case to convey something of the heart-arresting tension of
 a an important chess game.

From these examples you can understand why it is difficult
to lay down iron-clad rules for punctuation. Both examples are,
by literary standards, correct, compelling and readable, but in the
hands of lesser writers the extremes of 'over-stopping' and 'under-
stopping' are best avoided.

More important in good writing is when and where to use
the full stop. Take the following two thoughts:

● *The best store for sofas is Burton & Co.*

● *Our sofa has served us well for twenty years.*

Some writers might be tempted to link the two thoughts
to make a single sentence:

*Our sofa has served us well for twenty years, and the best
store for sofas is Burton & Co.*

A problem? Yes, because although the two thoughts are
related by a common subject – sofas – they really make two quite

separate points, and they don't marry at all well in a single sentence. The crudest way to deal with the problem is to express the thoughts by constructing *two* adjacent sentences – separated by a full stop:

> *Our sofa has served us well for twenty years. The best store for sofas is Burton & Co.*

But this solution feels uncomfortable, doesn't it? Although it is more logical and grammatically correct, we are left to ponder over the relationship between Burton & Co's sofa store and our serviceable 20-year old sofa. Where on earth is the connection? Was the sofa originally purchased from Burton & Co? If so, why not use this fact to link the two thoughts:

> *Our sofa has served us well for twenty years. It was supplied by Burton & Co, the best store for sofas.*

Or, dispensing with the full stop:

> *The sofa that's served us well for twenty years was supplied by Burton & Co, the best store for sofas.*

Fine, but what if the sofa had been purchased elsewhere? If this were the case, the presentation of the facts requires a different construction entirely. Perhaps something like this:

> *Although our sofa didn't come from Burton & Co, the best store for sofas, it has served us well for twenty years.*

A trio of tips about full stops and using them to form sentences:

- Keep your sentences variable in length, but generally short.

- Using long sentences doesn't necessarily make you a good writer.

- To use *only* full stops is as unnatural as hopping on one leg.

Full Stops and Abbreviations

Full stops have been used traditionally to shorten words, names and phrases. The convention was to use full stops for chopped-off words, or abbreviations:

doz. Sat. Oct. Prof. Staffs. lab. Inst. Fahr.

but not for shortenings consisting of the first and last letters of the word, or contractions:

Mr Dr gdn mfr St yd Revd wmk

Thus, by the rules, *per cent.* was considered to be an abbreviation because it chopped off the *'um'* from *per centum*. And while the *Rev. Golightly* required a full stop, the *Revd Golightly* didn't.

All this, however, has gone by the board because, increasingly and remorselessly, the stops are being abandoned in favour of speed, economy and cleaner typography. You will still see stops used for both abbreviations and contractions (for not everyone knows the difference) and sometimes to avoid ambiguity. Here is a sampling of the new order:

Formerly	**Now** (mostly)
6 a.m.	*6 am*
e.g.	*eg*
1472 A.D.	*1472 AD*
Jan. 16	*Jan 16*
Wm. Shakespeare	*Wm Shakespeare*
viz.	*viz*
R.S.V.P.	*RSVP*
Capt. Johns, D.F.C.	*Capt Johns, DFC*
U.K.	*UK*

Full stops are still required for certain other functional expressions:

- For money units: *£6.99, $99.89*

- For decimals: *20.86, 33.33%*

- For time (hours and minutes): *11.45am, 23.45 hrs*

The Common, but Contrary, Comma.

The comma is the most flexible, most versatile of all the punctuation marks. Because it is the least emphatic mark it is also the most subtle and complex. And contrary. Not surprisingly, many writers feel a nagging uncertainty about using commas.

While the full stop brings proceedings to a screeching halt, the comma, with its mortar-like ability to build complex sentences, enlarges upon thoughts, joins them to further thoughts and afterthoughts, binds in extra information, and generally has a good time. A writer with full command of the comma can have a ball. Here's the English humourist and columnist Alan Coren displaying an enviable skill in a passage in which the commas are like the carefully placed hoofprints of a horse lining up for a jump, and then – a long soaring comma-less passage follows before the full stop landing!

> *Until I was 40, I was utterly urban, uneasy in any surroundings more arborious than a sparsely tubbed patio, and knowing no more of wildlife than that a starling was probably taller than a stoat. As for the horse, I regarded it primarily as something to watch out for in French casseroles.*

> *But 40 is a critical age, a time for last-ditch stands, so I*
> *bought that last ditch in the New Forest, and the hovel that*
> *leaned over it, and enough land for the kids to run about and*
> *get tetanus in, somewhere, in short, which would allow me*
> *to escape into that sweet Arcadia where deer eat the rockery*
> *and mice eat the roof and ponies eat the hedges and a man*
> *can be snug in his nocturnal cot and hear naught but the*
> *soporific sound of death-watch beetles laughing at the*
> *inadequacy of creosote.*

Now that, to a comma freak, is about as good as you'll find anywhere in the language. Note, too, that Coren even gets away with a comma (after *get tetanus in, . . .*) where ordinary grammatically correct mortals would have placed a semicolon.

But back to earth. Perhaps the most resilient myth about commas is that they indicate natural breath pauses. There was a lot of truth in this, as we have seen, when the language was more orally inclined, but today commas have all but succumbed to grammatical logic.

> *Every year over the British Isles, half a million meteorites*
> *enter the atmosphere.*

You can hear the speaker intoning this, can't you – with a dramatic pause before announcing the impressive statistic *half a million*. Try it. But when you write it down as a sentence you find that the comma is redundant:

> *Every year over the British Isles half a million meteorites*
> *enter the atmosphere.*

Most writing today demands that commas be logical, but if you are a novelist, reporting a character's speech, you would be correct to use what are called 'rhetorical commas' when the character takes a breath.

Contemporary writing is far less rambling and rhetorical than it was in Dickens' day. Here's a not untypical sentence from *Martin Chuzzlewit*:

> *Then there was George Chuzzlewit, a gay bachelor cousin, who claimed to be young, but had been younger, and was inclined to corpulency, and rather overfed himself – to the extent, indeed, that his eyes were strained in their sockets, as if with constant surprise; and he had such an obvious disposition to pimples, that the bright spots on his cravat, the rich pattern on his waistcoat, and even his glittering trinkets, seemed to have broken out on him, and not to have come into existence comfortably.*

Tot up the commas – twelve in all, plus a dash and a semicolon. If you were disposed to attempt such a sentence today you would probably use only five commas, six at most. Whether it would retain the magic, though, is another matter. Try it.

Too, many, commas . . .

The over-use of commas still survives in sentences wrought by writers, possibly Librans, who can't make their minds up. Their sentences tend to be hedged with *ifs*, *buts*, *maybes* and pontifications:

It is, curiously, surprising when, say, you hear your name
announced in a foreign language, or even in a foreign accent.

Here's another example, from *The Times* a few years ago:

It is, however, already plain enough that, unless, indeed,
some great catastrophe should upset all their calculations . . .

It's grammatical, but a real pain to the reader. In most cases such sentences can be written with half the number of commas or less. Here's an over-spiced sentence which can be rewritten without any commas at all:

He had not, previously, met the plaintiff, except when, in
1984, he had, unexpectedly, found himself in Paris.

Those are bad cases of what the Fowler brothers, in *The King's English*, called 'spot plague' and fortunately, perhaps through the influence of newspaper brevity and the crispness of much modern fiction, they're a dying breed. But the injection of the single comma into a perfectly good sentence, simply because a writer feels it is lonely without one, is a growth industry:

- *The trophy presented to the winner, was the one*
  donated by the village butcher.

- *The gang left him, bleeding by the roadside.*

- *You can never foretell, what the weather will be*
  like.

Before we get too glib about unnecessary commas, here's a well-comma'd, heavily parenthesised sentence written by a craftsman, detective story writer Julian Symons. In this case you will find it rather difficult to remove any of the commas without causing confusion or disturbing the flow:

> *Waugh had already perfected his technique in writing dialogue, by which fragmented, interjectory, often apparently irrelevant, but, in fact, casually meaningful conversations carry along much of the plot, avoiding the need for description.*

The Comma Weight Reduction Plan

Piling on commas is as easy as putting on calories; in both cases the problem is getting rid of them. And if we do decide to slim, let's not go over the top. Here's an exercise in comma reduction, starting with a simple sentence that's gained a little too much weight:

A   *My hobby, trainspotting, is, to many, a joke.*

B   *My hobby, trainspotting, is to many, a joke.*

C   *My hobby, trainspotting, is to many a joke.*

D   *My hobby trainspotting, is to many a joke.*

E   *My hobby trainspotting is to many a joke.*

Pedants might claim that all five sentences differ in nuances of meaning, but to the average reader they all mean the same thing. So we are left with choosing which one is fit and lean enough to express our thought clearly, economically and elegantly. Which version would you choose? (our choice would be **C**, but it is our personal preference and not one we would wish to impose on others.)

The ability to recognise where commas are needed and where they are not may be an acquired skill but it is worth pursuing. Merely scanning a sentence will usually tell you. The writer of the following sentence was either afraid of commas or intent on speed of delivery:

The land is I believe owned by the City Council.

Most of us would place commas before and after the phrase *I believe* because it is an important qualifier; it needs to be highlighted from the main statement, *The land is . . . owned by the City Council* which, without the qualification, may or may not be true:

The land is, I believe, owned by the City Council.

A more serious lapse occurs when the lack of commas leads to ambiguity. A well-known illustration of this involves the fate of a young warrior in Ancient Greece who, on the eve of departing for a war, consults the Oracle at Delphi. *Thou shalt go thou shalt return never by war shalt thou perish*, he was told breathlessly. Mentally placing the commas after *go* and *return*, the warrior leapt on his chariot with brimming confidence. Unfortunately he was killed in the first battle without realising that what the Oracle meant was, *Thou shalt go, thou shalt return never, by war shalt thou perish*. Two commas could have saved his life.

One of the most common instances of the 'dropped comma' occurs when we write or utter the phrase *'No thanks'* – without separating or mentally separating the two words with a comma.

What we really mean is '*No* (I decline), *thanks*' (but thank you all the same); what we are in fact saying is '*No thanks*!' – which if you think about it is nothing less than a rude rejection!

As a general rule, where dropping a comma doesn't endanger understanding but instead helps the flow of the sentence, leave it out.

The Comma Splice

Another common error is the so-called **comma splice** – the use of a comma in place of a linking word to unite two sentences in the mistaken belief that it will form a single sentence:

The house is large, it has seven bedrooms.

That is not a grammatical sentence, but there are several ways to make it one:

● *The house is large; it has seven bedrooms.*

● *The house is large as it has seven bedrooms.*

● *The house is large and includes seven bedrooms.*

● *The house is large, with seven bedrooms.*

Simple? You would think so, but splicing a second sentence to another with an inadequate comma is not confined to the inexperienced writer. Here's the novelist E M Forster in *A Passage to India*:

*Chance brought her into his mind while it was in this heated
state, he did not select her, she happened to occur among the
throng of soliciting images, a tiny splinter, and he impelled
her by his spiritual force to that place where completeness can
be found.*

One hesitates to correct a master, but surely a full stop is
called for after *heated state*, and either a colon or semicolon after
select her. But you really begin to wonder when you find the great
stylist W Somerset Maugham scattering comma splices throughout
the pages of his novel *Of Human Bondage*:

*. . . often he sat and looked at the branches of a tree
silhouetted against the sky, it was like a Japanese print . . .
'You must congratulate me, I got my signatures yesterday . . .'
'I looked in on my way out, I wanted to tell you my news . . . '*

All three splices call for remedial action, with the commas
replaced by full stops, or at the very least by semicolons. In the last
two sentences linking words such as *for*, *because* or *as* could happily
substitute for the commas.

Correct Comma Placement

Despite their faulty construction, at least the meaning of
those offending sentences was clear. That, however, can't be said
of the following group of miscreants where commas, or the lack
of them, result in ambiguity.

Do we mean *They were sick and tired of the seemingly
endless journey.*

40

or . . .	*They were sick, and tired of the seemingly endless journey.*
Do we mean	*Brenda and Ian didn't fall in love because they liked their privacy too much.*
or . . .	*Brenda and Ian didn't fall in love, because they liked their privacy too much.*
Do we mean	*At the Coronation, she heard, many of the guests had to stand for over six hours.*
or . . .	*At the Coronation she heard many of the guests had to stand for over six hours.*
Do we mean	*My son Frederick invented the whoopee cushion.*
or . . .	*My son, Frederick, invented the whoopee cushion.*

All four examples here are slightly subtler versions of the following old chestnuts:

> *The deer spun an arrow through its heart.*
> *The deer spun, an arrow through its heart.*
>
> *To be honest, cashiers don't go home late.*
> *To be honest cashiers, don't go home late.*

But to return to the four sets of alternatives. In the first, the simple addition of a comma after *sick* alters the meaning of the sentence dramatically. Without the comma the travellers are merely 'fed up', but with the comma they are in a far worse state.

In the case of Brenda and Ian, the first sentence could imply that Brenda and Ian *did* fall in love, but not for the reason that they liked their privacy. With a comma after *love*, however, it is clear that their budding relationship foundered because they were protective of their privacy.

At the Coronation, the sentence with the two commas suggests that she may or may not have been present at the event but had heard anyhow that guests had to stand for over six hours. The sentence without the commas leads us to believe – although it is not absolutely clear – that she *was* present at the Coronation where she'd heard about the plight of some of the guests. Both sentences are flawed by ambiguity and would benefit from reconstruction. But either scenario is made quite clear in these versions:

> *She had heard that during the Coronation many of the guests had to stand for over six hours.*
> *While attending the Coronation she'd heard that many of the guests had to stand for over six hours.*

The final example illustrates a trap most of us fall into from time to time. Although superficially both sentences seem to be saying the same thing, the commas that enclose Frederick send out a signal that tells us that *Frederick* is my *only* son, whereas in the first sentence he could be one of several sons. How come?

Because this is such a common comma problem it's worth exploring the grammatical reasoning behind it. In the first sentence the information we have about Frederick is restrictive in that it defines a *kind* of son – a son named Frederick. In other words, an extended sentence might say, *Of all my sons the one named*

Frederick invented the whoopee cushion. The second sentence, however, is non-defining; here the fact that the son is named Frederick is incidental and non-essential information, which is why it is parenthesised between commas. What an extended sentence might say in this instance is, *My son invented the whoopee cushion; his name is Frederick, by the way*.

These are perhaps light-hearted instances of comma problems but sometimes a meaning hanging on the presence or absence of commas can be of great significance. Read the following statement, first with the comma, and then without it. Who has the violent seizures caused by thunder, the invalid or the herdsman?

> *Jacob looks after a herd of cows owned by a chronic invalid who constantly yells at him (,) and has seizures of the most violent kind whenever there's thunder about.*

All Things Bright and Beautiful

One of the most loved hymns of the Christian church is *All Things Bright and Beautiful*. So why, since half a century ago, has one of the verses been omitted? The offending verse contains the line, referring to the rich man in his castle and the poor man at his gate, *God made them, high or lowly, and ordered their estate*. Many clergy appear to have misunderstood the role of the commas in this line, believing it to mean that God made some people rich and some poor – a fair assumption had the commas been absent. But the commas make clear that everyone, whether 'high or lowly', is cared for equally. Nor does *estate* mean property, as some suppose. When composing the hymn in 1848 Mrs Alexander used *estate* in the biblical sense of 'existence or state of being'. It is moot whether the innocent verse is the victim of political correctness or a general ignorance of punctuation.

The Many Functions of the Comma

Thus far we've looked at how we misuse and abuse the comma. Now let's be positive and see how commas can help us express ourselves with clarity and style.

The comma's broad function is to separate words, phrases and clauses in a sentence to help it to be understood – to divide a sentence into easily assimilated bite-sized pieces. We soon learn to recognise that commas signal the ends of word groups, and because they are always contained *within* sentences, we know that more is to follow.

That is the basic function of the comma, but there are many others.

● **SETTING OFF NAMES AND PERSONS:**

> *Are you meeting him tomorrow, John?*
> *Listen, Helen, I've had quite enough.*
> *And that, ladies and gentlemen, is that.*
> *Of course you can do it, you nitwit!*
> *Darling, don't you think you've gone too far?*

● **ITEMISING WORDS:**

> *Please place all towels, costumes, clothing, bags and valuables in the lockers provided.*

● **ITEMISING WORD GROUPS:**

> *Please place any articles of clothing, swimming and sporting equipment, personal belongings, but not money and jewellery in the lockers.*

- **ENCLOSING ADDITIONAL THOUGHTS OR QUALIFICATIONS:**

  The occasion was, on the whole, conducted with commendable dignity.
  The judges thought it was, arguably, one of his finest novels.

- **SETTING OFF INTERJECTIONS:**

  Look, I can't take any more of this!
  Blimey, isn't the beach crowded today?
  Stop, or I'll call the police.

- **SETTING OFF DIRECT SPEECH:**

  Jill turned abruptly and said, "If that's how you feel, then go home!"

- **SETTING OFF QUESTIONS:**

  You'll be going soon, won't you?
  She's marrying James tomorrow, isn't she?

- **EMPHASISING POINTS OF VIEW:**

  Naturally, I'll look after your new car.
  Of course, she fully deserves the prize.

- **SETTING OFF COMPARATIVE OR CONTRASTING STATEMENTS:**

  The taller they are, the farther they fall.
  The more he said he adored Maisie, the less they cared.

- **REINFORCING STATEMENTS:**

    She's ill because she won't eat, that's why!
    It'll come right in the end, I'm sure.

- **REPLACING MISSING WORDS:**

    If you want more time, half an hour, maximum.
    [you can have]

- **SETTING OFF AN INTRODUCTORY WORD OR PHRASE:**

    Sausages, which are far from fat free, pose a problem for
    dieters.

Omitting the opening comma required to separate a
subordinate clause (*which are far from fat free*) from the main clause
(*Sausages . . . pose a problem for dieters*) is a common mistake, and one
that usually leads to ambiguity. With the commas correctly in
place, as in our example, we are in no doubt that the description
far from fat free applies to *all* sausages. But omit that opening
comma and a different meaning can be conveyed: *Sausages which
are far from fat free, pose a problem for dieters*. Now the statement is
saying that only those sausages that are *far from fat free* are a
problem. But if that is what is actually meant, the remaining
comma is redundant.

Here's another example, from *The Times*:

    Overnight fans had painted messages on the road outside his
    home . . . "We love you Frank".

Overnight fans? Are these different from ordinary fans? Obviously a comma after the introductory scene-setting word *Overnight* is required to make things clear.

Using Commas with Adjectives

Using commas to form lists of nouns and names is, as we've seen, quite straightforward. We don't say, for example,

Bill and Jean and Marcus and Chloe went out riding.

or

Bill Jean Marcus and Chloe went out riding.

but

Bill, Jean, Marcus and Chloe went out riding.

A similar list of adjectives, used to modify a noun or proper noun, requires a little more care. See if you can work out, in the following two sentences, why one has the adjectives separated by commas, and the other does not:

- *The night resounded with a loud, chilling, persistent ringing.*

- *It was a large brick Victorian mansion.*

The reasons are embodied in two seemingly simple rules worth remembering:

● Where the adjectives (or other modifiers) define
  <u>separate</u> attributes (*loud, chilling, persistent*),
  they are best separated by commas.

● Where the adjectives work together to create a
  single image (*large, brick, Victorian*), the commas
  are often best omitted.

Two seemingly simple rules, but they can be tricky to apply.
The late, great grammarian Sir Ernest Gowers was never too bothered
about commas between adjectives, quoting as equally correct:

'a silly, verbose, pompous letter'

and

'a silly verbose pompous letter'

and adding that the commas in this case merely added emphasis
to the adjectives.

Nevertheless, comma placement between adjectives can lead
to ambiguity. An undergraduate joke used to concern a popular
song title: *What is This Thing Called Love?* Place a comma between
Called and *Love* and you have an intriguing ambiguity. A comma
can make all the difference, as in:

A pretty smart young lady.
A pretty, smart young lady.

In the first statement the adjective *pretty* attaches itself to the next adjective *smart*, to mean something between 'fairly smart' and 'very smart'; moreover it makes no reference to the young lady's appearance. The second statement, however, means that here we have an attractive young lady who is also smart.

One way to deal with the ambiguity problem is to imagine an *and* between the adjectives; if an *and* can be inserted and still make sense, then a comma can normally be substituted:

*Tracy was a young **and** exciting photographic model.*
Tracy was a young, exciting photographic model.

Now let us look at a sentence where inserting an and would be plainly silly:

Tracy was a beautiful young photographic model.
*Tracy was a beautiful **and** young photographic model.*

This sentence, with or without a comma between *beautiful* and *young*, would mean the same thing, but a comma would be an irritant to eye and ear and mind because it would split what should be a single image: '*beautiful young*'.

We're not talking about grammatical exactitude here but simple logic and common sense. Often, merely 'listening' to your writing will guide you. Here's a multi-adjective construction utilising a single comma. Would you settle for that, or use more?

She wore the eye-catching Parisian blue silk Molyneaux
bridal dress flown in only yesterday, with her customary flair.

Commas with Adverbs and Adverbial Phrases

It is customary to use commas to enclose modifying adverbs and adverbial phrases such as *however, indeed, nevertheless, in fact, needless to say, no doubt, incidentally, anyway, for example, on the contrary, of course* and *as we have seen*:

*You are, **nevertheless**, guilty of the first charge.*

Increasingly, however, [notice the enclosing commas!] such commas are dropped when the meaning remains clear without them:

*You are **nevertheless** guilty of the first charge.*

But be alert for ambiguity: *The hospital informed us that both victims were, happily, recovering.* Remove the enclosing commas either side of *happily* and you'd give the impression that the victims were not only recovering but having the time of their lives! And see, in the next example, reporting on a parliamentary debate about field sports, how vital a pair of enclosing commas can be:

Mr Douglas Hogg said that he had shot, himself, as a small boy.

Commas are also needed for sentences beginning with adverbs:

>   ***Curiously,*** *the two cousins had never met.*
>   ***Ironically,*** *they discovered they were sisters.*
>   ***Looking scared,*** *Peter peered out of the window.*

and also for sentences containing adverbial clauses:

>   *Peter,* ***not usually given to heroics****, smartly lowered his head.*

Other Problem Comma Placements

Sometimes you will find that verbs will need enclosing by commas to help guide readers through a complex passage:

>   *In the daytime,* ***sleeping****, the baby was adorable, but at nights,* ***howling continuously****, she was a tyrant and a monster.*

For the same reason a clarifying comma is usually required to separate two conjunctions:

>   *Norma asked* ***whether****,* ***if*** *the register was in the church, she might look up her family records.*

You can see the necessity for using separating commas in sentences such as those above. The same applies to a build-up of prepositions:

>   *The helicopter hovered* ***in****,* ***around****,* ***over*** *and finally* ***through*** *the eerie pink cloud.*

One of the most common sentence constructions is frequently marred by confusion about where to place a comma:

Jeremy glanced at the clock, and abruptly closing his book, leapt up from the sofa.

There's something vaguely amiss with this, isn't there? What's amiss is that the comma should follow the *and*, not precede it. To understand and correct this, we must separate the two structural components of the sentence, the main clause (*Jeremy glanced at the clock and . . . leapt up from the sofa*) and the subordinate clause (*abruptly closing his book*) to discover where the *and* really belongs. When we find it belongs to the main clause we can place the comma in the correct position. So the sentence should read:

Jeremy glanced at the clock and, abruptly closing his book, leapt up from the sofa.

or

Jeremy glanced at the clock, and, abruptly closing his book, leapt up from the sofa.

Although placing commas before, after or around *and* is pretty much a matter of grammatical logic, with other conjunctions it isn't so straightforward. The American writer Margaret Mitchell had a superb ear for punctuation and her comma placements have been widely studied. Here, for example, is a sentence from *Gone with the Wind* with three variations of comma placement around the conjunction *for*:

A *The mismanagement of the state road especially
infuriated the taxpayers, for, out of the earnings of
the road, was to come the money for free schools.*

B *The mismanagement of the state road especially
infuriated the taxpayers for, out of the earnings of
the road, was to come the money for free schools.*

C *The mismanagement of the state road especially
infuriated the taxpayers, for out of the earnings of
the road was to come the money for free schools.*

Grammatically, **A** is the more correct version; **C** would be
preferred by most writers today; **B** is Margaret Mitchell's original.
Yet all, except perhaps by ultra-pedantic standards, are acceptable.

The Oxford, or Final Comma

The Times advises its journalists to 'avoid the so-called
Oxford comma: *x, y and z* and not *x, y, and z*.'
What this means is that:

Martin spoke to Edith, Lesley, Bunty and Samantha.
is preferred to
Martin spoke to Edith, Lesley, Bunty, and Samantha.

Sound advice; a final comma before *and* in a list
is now outmoded – unless there is the possibility
of ambiguity:

The colours of the flag are red, green and gold in stripes.

What does this mean? Red and green, with gold stripes?
Red, green and gold stripes? Red, with green and gold
stripes? What the sentence needs is a comma for clarity.
If, as intended, the statement was meant to describe a flag
consisting of just three bold stripes, it should say so:
The colours of the flag are red, green, and gold, in stripes.

Using Commas to Parenthesise

One of the most interesting, but also perhaps the most contentious, use of commas, is to parenthesise (or place in parenthesis) relevant but not essential matter from the main part of the sentence:

The wild hyacinths (which are at the height of the season) tint the woods with a blue mist.

The essential message here is: *The wild hyancinths tint the woods with a pale blue mist.* But we've had a further thought – *which are now at the height of their season* – which we'd like to include in the same sentence. Sometimes we enclose such additions in parentheses (brackets) as above, but mostly we use a pair of far more convenient and less disruptive commas:

*The wild hyacinths, **which are now at the height of their season**, tint the woods with a pale blue mist.*

When you parenthesise it's important to remember that the commas *always work in pairs* – an opening comma and a closing comma:

WRONG *He wrote the year's biggest bestseller, 'Storm Over Jackdaw Bay' in just over three months.*

CORRECT *He wrote the year's biggest bestseller, 'Storm Over Jackdaw Bay', in just over three months.*

Although understanding the role of commas in isolating subordinate statements is easy enough, there are traps, as in this piece of nonsense:

56

The two lead actors, who appear in 'Grease', won their respective roles after many gruelling years in musicals.

The two enclosing commas here are telling us that *who appear in 'Grease'* is non-essential information. But if you rewrite the sentence without that phrase it makes no sense: we don't know who the lead actors are or what they are doing. In fact, *who appear in 'Grease'* is a defining or restrictive phrase – one that identifies, modifies or qualifies its subject. It is essential, not non-essential, information. So the sentence should read:

The two lead actors who appear in 'Grease' won their respective roles after many gruelling years in musicals.

This amended sentence, with an absence of any parenthesised or subordinate matter, signals to us that we must read every word to get the meaning. That's why it's important to get it right. Here's an example from a newspaper that got it wrong:

In 1991 the witness testified he was never in this country.

What the newspaper meant to say was:

*In 1991, **the witness testified**, he was never in this country.*

The first sentence tells us clearly that the witness was never in this country, ever – he testified to that effect in 1991. In fact, the man lived in this country, but claimed in court in 1996 that in 1991 he'd been abroad. Big difference.

Or take the case of the migratory salmon:

A   *Salmon which can leap heights of up to fifteen feet scoop furrows in upstream reaches to deposit their spawn.*

B   *Salmon, which can leap heights of up to fifteen feet, scoop furrows in upstream reaches to deposit their spawn.*

Sentence **B** tells us that all salmon – which incidentally can leap up to fifteen feet – spawn upstream. Sentence **A**, on the other hand, is concerned only with those lucky, super-sexed salmon that can leap fifteen feet to reach the spawning grounds. Bad luck about the others.

There are of course other constructions that allow us to sideline subsidiary thoughts and secondary information with commas. Sometimes we might wish to add more importance or force to a subordinate statement; this can be done by highlighting it at the front of a sentence, or adding it as a 'sting in the tail':

A   *The lawn grass mixture, however fast it might grow, turns brown with the slightest drought.*

B   *However fast it might grow, the lawn grass mixture turns brown with the slightest drought.*

C   *The lawn grass mixture turns brown with the slightest drought, however fast it might grow.*

Of these, **A** is the blandest while **C**, with its forthright statement up front and dismissive comment at the end, is the most condemnatory of the lawn grass mixture.

To summarise:

- Where a phrase or clause does not define or
  qualify the subject, indicate that it is non-essential
  matter by isolating it with a pair of commas.

- Where a phrase or clause defines or qualifies the
  subject, unite it with the subject by omitting the
  commas.

- When you need to place more emphasis on
  subordinate matter, try other constructions.

The Serviceable Semicolon

From the long pause (full stop) and the short pause (comma) we now come to the linking pauses in between: the semicolon and the colon. Of these two the colon is the weightier, and older by a century or so than its sibling, which was introduced around 1650. Despite their age, both marks are still widely misunderstood, misused – and shunned. Let's first explore the uses of the semicolon.

It would be easy to define a semicolon as half a colon, but that's hardly a useful description. To say that a semicolon is a pause somewhere between a strong comma and a weak full stop is nearer the mark, but this still lacks precision and purpose. A more formal and grammatical definition is Hart's: 'The semicolon separates two or more clauses which are of more or less equal importance and are linked as a pair or series: *To err is human; to forgive, divine.*''

That said, the fact remains that using semicolons involves a greater degree of judgment than that required by any of the other marks. Consider the following statement in four versions:

A   *He was once a dunce at maths. Now he's a professor of mathematics.*

B   *He was once a dunce at maths now he's a professor of mathematics.*

C   *He was once a dunce at maths, now he's a professor of mathematics.*

D   *He was once a dunce at maths but now he's a professor of mathematics.*

You'll see immediately that versions **B** and **C** are grammatically incorrect; **B** lacks a break between the two separate statements, and **C** attempts to achieve it – wrongly – with a 'comma splice'. There's nothing wrong with **A** except that it's two sentences which, with a bit of work, could economically be made into one. Version **D** is fine although a stylist might pronounce it rather flat.

What, though, are the statements trying to say? The facts are that here's someone who was once hopeless at maths and who, years later, has become a professor of mathematics. Isn't that surprising? Even amazing? And not a little ironical? And that's what not one of the four versions manages to convey – the unlikely outcome, the ironical result. The facts are all in place but somehow the real point of the statements doesn't hit home.

Of course the facts could be rewritten to make the point but, before we do this, is there a form of punctuation that might enable us to project the surprise and irony? As a matter of fact, there is: the semicolon:

E   *He was once a dunce at maths; now he's a professor of mathematics.*

Done! The semicolon not only links the two independent but related statements (which a comma can't do without a conjunction) in a grammatically correct way but it also emphasises the incongruity as a bonus. One small step for a semicolon, one giant leap for punctuation.

The Dejected, Rejected Semicolon

Quite a few experienced writers are honest enough to admit to having never completely mastered the semicolon, finding it the most difficult punctuation mark to use correctly. Some, like George Orwell, actually developed a hatred for them. In one of his novels, *Coming Up For Air* (1939), Orwell managed to exclude the semicolon altogether, although three did creep in only to be thrown out in a later edition. More recently, Martin Amis managed to reduce his semicolon quota to a single one in his novel *Money* (1984). George Bernard Shaw complained of T E Lawrence that while he threw colons about like a madman he hardly used semicolons at all. Indeed, the heat provoked by the anti-semicolonists some years ago led to fears that the mark would become an endangered species, and a Society for the Preservation of the Semicolon was formed.

Such quirkiness is unjustified. Despite its dismissal by many writers and teachers the semicolon is a very clever punctuation tool with a number of important grammatical and stylistic functions.

The Functions of the Semicolon

- To join words, word groups and sentences.

- To separate word groups that already contain commas.

- To restore order in sentences suffering from 'Comma Riot'.

- To provide pauses before certain adverbs.

- To emphasise contrasts and incongruity.

- **Using semicolons to join words, word groups and sentences.**

Occasionally we find ourselves writing a long sentence with too many connecting words such as *and, but* and *also*, with the danger of getting into an impossible tangle:

> *The history of the semicolon and colon is one of confusion because there are no precise rules governing their use and, furthermore, many writers would argue that both marks are really stylistic rather than parenthetical devices, and can in any case be easily replaced by commas, stops and dashes, and there the argument rests.*

There's nothing grammatically wrong with that but it is unwieldy and unappealing to both eye and mind. Many writers would, without hesitation, recast it as two or more separate sentences:

> *The history of the semicolon and colon is one of confusion. There are no precise rules governing their use. Many writers argue that both marks are really stylistic rather than parenthetical devices which can easily be replaced by commas, stops and dashes. And there the argument rests.*

We have previously seen how the judicious use of full stops to achieve shorter sentences can aid understanding, and that certainly is the case here. But some writers, feeling that the original long sentence is, after all, about a single subject and should therefore be kept as a whole and not split apart, would turn to the semicolon to achieve unity of thought without making things hard for the reader:

> *The history of the semicolon and colon is one of confusion; there are no precise rules governing their use; many writers argue that both marks are really stylistic rather than parenthetical devices and that they can easily be replaced by commas, stops and dashes; and there the argument rests.*

The use of semicolons to link single words is rarely called for, but here for the record is an example: *Birth; life; death: three certainties in an uncertain world.*

● To separate word groups containing commas.

Any sentence that is essentially a list should be crystal clear and easily read. Most 'sentence lists' adequately separate the items with commas, but sometimes the items themselves are word groups containing commas and require semicolons for clarity. These two examples illustrate how useful semicolons can accomplish this task:

> ● *Those present included Mr and Mrs Allison, their daughters Sarah, Megan and Sue; the Smith twins; Reg and Paul Watson; Joyce, Helen and Bill Hobson; Major and Mrs Dickson; etc.*

● *The Chicago band lineup consisted of Bix Beiderbecke, cornet; Al Grande, trombone; George Johnson and Peck Jones, tenor sax; Bob Gillette, banjo; Dick Voynow, piano, and Vic Moore on drums.*

● **To restore order to sentences suffering from 'Comma Riot'.**

Here's a longish but reasonably accomplished sentence spoiled by 'comma riot':

His main aims in life, according to Wilma, were to achieve financial independence, to be powerfully attractive, not only to women in general but in particular to rich ladies, to eat and drink freely without putting on weight, to remain fit, vital and young-looking beyond his eightieth birthday and, last but not least, to not only read, but fully understand, Professor Stephen Hawking's 'A Brief History of Time'.

Many professional writers would defend that sentence, despite its eleven commas. But others, perhaps more concerned with clarity than with rhythm, would suggest that some of the thoughts at least should be separated by the longer pauses provided by semicolons:

> *His main aims in life, according to Wilma, were to achieve financial independence; to be powerfully attractive, not only to women in general but in particular to rich ladies; to eat and drink freely without putting on weight; to remain fit, vital and young-looking beyond his eightieth birthday and, last but not least, to not only read but fully understand Professor Stephen Hawking's 'A Brief History of Time'.*

● **To provide pauses before certain adverbs.**

There are certain adverbs and conjunctions that require a preceding pause, but one longer and stronger than that provided by a comma. Look at this example:

WITH A COMMA   *It was a superb car, moreover it was economical to run.*

WITH A SEMICOLON   *It was a superb car; moreover it was economical to run.*

You can see and, more importantly, *hear*, that need for a substantial pause before *moreover*, can't you? A comma is wrong on both grammatical and rhetorical counts. Here's another example; read it aloud and note your instinctive pause before *nevertheless*:

> *Joe claimed he'd beaten the bookies on every race; nevertheless he was broke as usual when he left the track.*

Watch out for *therefore, however, also, moreover, furthermore, hence, consequently* and *subsequently*; in many constructions they will require a preceding semicolon.

● **To emphasise contrasts and incongruity.**

At the beginning of this chapter we saw an example of how a semicolon was used to heighten an ironical statement. Skilled writers have long exploited this function: the semicolon's ability to administer mild shock or censure; to highlight absurdity and contradiction; to leave a self-deprecating afterthought. In the latter mode, here is Henry Thoreau in *Walden*:

> *I had more visitors while I lived in the woods than at any other period in my life; I mean that I had some.*

Here's a more piquant example. For a woman to remark, 'I thought his wife was lovely, but her dress was in poor taste' would be fairly pedestrian and certainly lacking in feminine acuity. Here's what she might wish she'd said with the tart use of a mental semicolon:

> *I loved his wife; pity about the frock.*

One of the most enthusiastic users of the semicolon in literature was undoubtedly Charles Dickens, who even used them, unusually, to parenthesise, usurping the role of brackets or dashes:

> *Such was the account; rapidly furnished in whispers, and interrupted, brief as it was, by many false alarms of Mr Pecksniff's return; which Martin received of his godfather's decline.*

Most writers today would of course isolate the parenthetical matter with an opening bracket or dash before *rapidly* and a closing bracket or dash after *return*. More conventionally, here is Dickens in full semicolonic flight, again, in *Martin Chuzzlewit*:

> *There were two bottles of currant wine, white and red; a dish of sandwiches (very long and very slim); another of apples; another of captain's biscuits (which are always a moist and jovial sort of viand); a plate of oranges cut up small and gritty, with powdered sugar; and a highly geological home-made cake. The magnitude of these preparations quite took away Tom Pinch's breath: for though the new pupils were usually let down softly, as one may say, particularly in the wine department, which had so many stages of declension, that sometimes a young gentleman was a whole fortnight in getting to the pump; still this was a banquet; a sort of Lord Mayor's feast in private life; a something to think of, and hold on by, afterwards.*

A Semicolon Self-test

To prove to yourself that you've grasped the principles of using semicolons, try these exercises. The recommended versions will be found on the page overleaf. Some of the test examples will need recasting while one or two invite you to choose between commas and semicolons.

1   *Everyone is wary of the cliff; the face of which has weathered alarmingly.*

2   *The couple scarcely knew anyone, and were slow to form friendships; having little enthusiasm for new faces.*

3   *It should be stressed that Stephanie's behaviour is unacceptable, it should be brought to her notice immediately.*

4   *The Austen household consisted of a cook, laundress, two maids and a butler, a groom and watchman and a head gardener and under-gardener.*

5   *Having lost his job in the recession, having had the ill-luck to lose his home and possessions to the bank, having, on top of everything, his wife leave him, Patrick was perhaps justified in feeling bitter.*

Semicolon Self-test:
Answers and Discussion

1. A comma is all that's required as the *cliff* and its *face* are so closely related. You could rewrite it as:

    Everyone is wary of the cliff-face, which has weathered alarmingly.

2. Much the same applies to this example, in which the first comma can be deleted as redundant, and a comma substituted for the semicolon:

    The couple scarcely knew anyone and were slow to form friendships, having little enthusiasm for new faces.

3. Here you have two quite separate though related thoughts, requiring a pause longer and stronger than a comma. You could join the two thoughts economically with a semicolon but many writers might prefer to use a comma and a conjunction, such as *and*:

    It should be stressed that Stephanie's behaviour is unacceptable, and it should be brought to her notice immediately.

4. The reader can be easily confused here. Is *a groom and watchman* one person doing both jobs, or two individual employees? Use semicolons to make the sentence clear and easy to follow:

The Austen household consisted of a cook, laundress, two maids and a butler; a groom; a watchman; and a head gardener and under-gardener.

5. There is nothing grammatically or stylistically wrong with this complex sentence although, if there is a weakness, it lies in the crack between *bank* and *having* where many writers might feel the need for a break more pronounced than a comma. Here's the sentence again, a little more pedantically constructed and not, in everyone's eyes, necessarily an improvement:

Having lost his job in the recession; having had the ill-luck to lose his home and possessions to the bank; and having, on top of everything, his wife leave him – Patrick was perhaps justified in feeling bitter.

Trouble with your Colon?

The colon is an old punctuation mark. Introduced in the 16th century it virtually disappeared for a time during the 19th, only to be rescued from near oblivion in the 20th. Now, as we approach the 21st century, it's under threat from the dash.

It is a mark often casually tossed aside, and many people write passable prose without ever feeling the need to use it. So why bother?

Well, you can cook without salt, too, or wear shoes without socks or stockings. Just as some relatively minor details can enrich your quality of life, so can the colon enhance the quality of your writing.

In fact the colon is a versatile workhorse, and many colon-scoffers are stopped in their tracks when confronted with the range of its functions.

But, first, there are three useful points to remember about colons:

- The difference between a semicolon and a colon is not a difference in weight or force; the two marks are mostly used for quite different purposes.

- Generally, the colon takes the reader's interest forward: from introduction to main subject, from cause to effect, from premise to conclusion.

- A colon is never followed by a capital letter, except when the following word is a proper noun or the first word of an independent quotation.

The Functions of the Colon

So far, hundreds of colons have been used to punctuate the text of this book, for a variety of purposes. Here's a comprehensive list of the ways in which we can make them work for us:

1   To point the reader's attention forward.

2   To introduce a list.

3   To present an explanation or example.

4   To introduce direct speech.

5   To present a conclusion.

6   To introduce a quotation.

7   To introduce a question.

8   To link contrasting statements.

9   To substitute for a conjunction.

10 To introduce a subtitle.

There are a few more functions explained at the end of the chapter but, meanwhile, here are some examples of the colon in everyday use.

● To point the reader's attention forward.

In this role the colon acts as a pointing finger, as if to warn the reader about a statement ahead: *Wait for it . . . here it comes!* Or, in the more eloquent words of the grammarian Henry Fowler, its function is 'that of delivering the goods that have been invoiced in the preceding words'. The 'goods' might be a conclusion, a summary, a list or a contrasting statement:

> *Maddeningly beautiful, honey-voiced, overwhelmingly generous, owner of three luxury homes and a ranch in Texas: she was a glittering prize for any man.*

● To introduce a list.

This is the workhorse role of most colons:

> *The hotel had everything: pool, sauna, Jacuzzi, gym, hairdresser, tanning booths and even a dietician.*

> *Detective Stevens entered and took it all in: the body, the still smouldering mattress, the cigarette ends on the floor . . .*

● To present an explanation or example.

> *The beleaguered bank closed its doors for good after just a month in business: not surprising when you saw the list of directors.*

Introductory words and phrases such as *namely, as follows* and *for example* (and *eg*) are often followed by colons:

There are three reasons why Lainston House near Winchester is an outstanding restaurant, namely: excellent cuisine, superbly restored interiors, and super-attentive staff.

● **To introduce direct speech.**

Although many stylists insist that commas are the correct marks for introducing direct speech (see chapter on the **Comma**, page 33), the use of colons for this purpose nowadays hardly earns a frown:

The Mayor strode to the platform, opened his notes and glared at the assembly: 'You've not come here tonight just to listen to me,' he growled.

● **To present a conclusion.**

Fifty-five years in the business suggested to old Jake that there was only one certainty in life: the inevitability of change.

The fact that Ernest's right hand never knew what his left was doing had an unfortunate effect on his life: he could never hold down a job.

● **To introduce a quotation.**

Rachel's thoughts were neatly summed up by Swift: 'That flattery's the food of fools . . . Yet now and then your men of wit will condescend to take a bit'.

Gradually, one by one, Arnold's words came back to me: 'And we forget because we must, and not because we will'.

● **To introduce a question.**

Although commas can be used to set off a question in a
sentence, the colon is preferred by most writers:

> *They all agreed that the essential issue was simply this: did*
> *she or did she not seduce Sir Timothy in the stable block?*

● **To link contrasting statements.**

In this role the colon shares with the semicolon the ability
to create surprise and shock, and underline irony. The choice is
based on emphasis: use a semicolon when the concluding
statement is more an aside or afterthought (see examples in the
chapter on the **semicolon**); and a colon when it is an abrupt,
unarguable conclusion:

> *Jeremy had just one disconcerting fault: he was an inveterate*
> *liar.*

> *Her love affair with her son's school, its history, its*
> *achievements, its famous alumni and its crumbling charm*
> *would have endured for ever but for one consideration:*
> *the £12,000 yearly fees.*

> *She cooks: I eat.*

● **To substitute for a conjunction.**

In the following example, the writer preferred the punchier
colon to a choice of conjunctions such as **and** or **so**:

Rodriguez downed the champ with a dazzling left hook that came out of nowhere: Hayman did not get up.

● **To introduce a subtitle.**

Men at War: An Introduction to Chess.

Gilbert White: Observer in God's Little Acre.

● **Other sundry uses of the colon.**

Despite all the functions described so far, we haven't yet finished with this useful mark. If you ever read a stageplay, you'll often find it laid out something like this:

GEORGE:	*You've said enough –*
ANNA:	*I haven't even started!*
GEORGE:	*Enough! D'you hear me!*

Then there is the 'biblical' colon, separating chapter and verse (*Ecclesiastes 3:12*); the mathematical colon used to express ratios (*Male athletes outnumber females by 3:2*); and the time colon (*The train departs at 12:45*). In the US it is customary to use colons to open a letter: *Dear Anna: I do look forward to seeing you soon . . .*

Misuse of the Colon

Perhaps because many people steer clear of colons, abuse of the mark is comparatively rare. But it does exist, not least in newspapers:

77

The man was amazing and was able to play: the piano, violin, double-bass, trombone, clarinet, saxophone, harp and drums.

This is a plain case of redundant colon; if you listen to the sentence you'll instantly agree that it reads better without any mark or pause between *play* and the *piano*.

Here's another instance where use of a colon leads only to confusion:

Today's English cherry, however, is likely to be Canadian in origin, bred to be split-resistant and grown on dwarf rootstocks: 11 or 12ft high.

The unnecessary colon leads us to believe that the rootstocks are 11 or 12ft high – which can hardly be described as 'dwarf'! What is apparently meant is that the *entire* tree is 11 to 12ft high, in which case the sentence ought to be reconstructed:

Today's English cherry, however, is likely to be Canadian in origin, bred to be split-resistant, and grown on dwarf rootstocks to keep the trees down to 11 or 12ft high.

This final example is a piece of compressed journalese:

The desperate Prime Minister was forced to axe Nadir victim Michael Mates [from the Cabinet] despite telling him privately: you've done nothing wrong.

The writer has, in the view of many, done nothing wrong, either; the colon is a versatile and optional mark. But its use here is ill-fitting and the sentence is clumsy.

Here is a suggested reconstruction:

The desperate Prime Minister was forced to axe Nadir victim Michael Mates despite telling him privately, 'You've done nothing wrong'.

The Seductive Embrace of Parentheses [Brackets]

In our discussion of commas we saw how supplementary material in a sentence could be set apart or **parenthesised** (the term **parenthesis**, via Latin and Greek, means 'an insertion besides') by enclosing it between a pair of commas.

The sentence above is just such an example, except that instead of using commas we have used a pair of brackets, or **round ( ) brackets**. But because round brackets are used solely for the purpose of *parenthesising* they are more correctly referred to as **parentheses** and the *parenthetical* matter contained between them is said to be in *parenthesis*. The functions of other types of brackets – [ ], { } and < > – are discussed later.

If you look at that first sentence again you will see that the parentheses serve to set apart relevant but supplementary matter which could, if you wished to be ruthless, be dropped altogether without changing the meaning of the sentence. If you did prune away those words, the sentence would still express the same thought, with an uninterrupted flow. But by retaining the words (in parenthesis) the sentence, and the reader, gain from the additional information.

So what's the difference between parenthesising material between commas and between parentheses? Generally, material within commas is still very much part of the sentence, and must observe the grammatical conventions of that sentence. Bracketed material, on the other hand, is rather more distanced from the sentence proper. Brackets also release the writer from a lot of responsibility as the parenthesised material, leading a separate life as it were, is not required grammatically to match the sentence into which it is inserted. Here, for example, is a parenthesised statement which posesses its own punctuation, independent of the enclosing sentence:

> *Although we've never seen a mole, their depredations in the garden (we counted over fifty molehills last Sunday, an increase of fifteen in just a week. And those were confined to the main lawn; there are hundreds more in the orchard) are all too evident.*

That insert is by most writing standards unacceptably long, but it does demonstrate the independence of bracketed text, and how it can play merry with grammatical rules. The first sentence begins without a capital letter and the second even dispenses with a full stop! Here's a shorter example demonstrating the convenience of the backet:

> *Julian, Maurice and George Marcus (George is the black sheep of the family, and an actor) were all at the reception.*

To convey precisely this information without brackets would require reconstructing the sentence, using commas to parenthesise the supplementary matter:

Julian and Maurice Marcus, and their brother George, the
black sheep of the family and an actor, were all at the reception.

We also have another option – substituting a pair of dashes for the brackets – which we'll discuss in the appropriate chapter later on.

You can see that for many writers brackets are a godsend; unfortunately these same writers are also prone to over-use them. The embrace of parentheses is seductive and promiscuous, as the following catalogue of examples of usage demonstrates:

ADDING INFORMATION *One of the earliest dictionaries which sets out to explain 'difficult terms' is that of Elisha Coles (Published in London, 1685).*

EXPLANATION *Unable to follow the French instructions and after nothing but trouble she returned the car (a Renault saloon) to the garage.*

AFTERTHOUGHT *During the tour they visited at least a dozen cities and towns (but why not, we wondered, Paris and Marseilles?) in just ten days.*

CLARIFICATION *The directive stated quite clearly (page 15, second paragraph) that the premises would be closed from March 1.*

COMMENT *The women of Brayville were refused admission (why? were they drunk and disorderly?) twice in the same day.*

ILLUSTRATION *The candidate spent far too long discussing irrelevancies (15 minutes on the high price of footwear; another ten on* *the evils of tax havens) with the result that most of his audience walked out and never returned.*

CONFIDENTIAL REMARK *We're finally leaving this place on Thursday (Oh, God! I can't wait!) and I'll write as soon as we reach Bombay.*

EXPRESSING AN ASIDE *Sylvia promises to lose three stones in just a month (and pigs will fly, too).*

INDICATING OPTIONS *Your document(s) will be forwarded to the prospective employer.*

EXPRESSING DOUBT *According to the magazine, Priscilla had always been the cleverest, sportiest, most-liked (?) girl in her class.*

You'll note that all these examples conform in two important ways:

- Take the parenthesised matter away and the sentence flows on unaffected.

- The parenthesised matter assumes its own punctuation, independent of that of the surrounding sentence.

Abusing the Bracket

Is it possible to misuse or abuse such a straightforward, easy-to-use punctuation mark? Misuse is relatively rare but abuse abounds. How often do we see parentheses bulging with the contents of fifty- or sixty-word mini-essays, so long that by the time we get to the end of them we've lost the drift of the main sentence? If you find yourself writing a parenthesised statement longer than a dozen or at most twenty words, stop and think about restructuring the sentence.

Here's an example of another form of bracket abuse, although more a stylistic sin than grammatical. It occurred in, of all places, a review of a book about punctuation:

> *Admittedly, punctuation has changed little since the middle of the 16th century, when the widespread dissemination of typefaces among the printers of Europe began to make standardisation possible.(The semicolon as we know it had taken root about 1494; the comma nearer 1520; the apostrophe in 1529.)*

So, what's wrong with that? For one thing it is difficult to justify the need for parenthesis anyway. The review ran in *The Times* which says in its *Style Guide* for journalists: 'Like capitals and dashes they [brackets] look ugly in a column of type and should be avoided wherever possible'. And, secondly, a bracketed afterthought isn't the most elegant way with which to close a sentence or a paragraph. Here's a suggested reconstruction, without the parentheses:

> *Admittedly, punctuation has changed little since the middle of the 16th century; the semicolon as we know it had taken root about 1494, the comma nearer 1520 and the apostrophe in 1529; after which the widespread dissemination of typefaces among the printers of Europe began to make standardisation possible.*

Even less justified is the following parenthesised appendage which, again, occurred in a book review. You can see immediately that the brackets are wholly redundant:

> *'Killing Ground' is the story of the Battle of the Atlantic,*
> *a full-scale war, with no rules and no mercy. (It is also the*
> *story of the destroyer, HMS Gladiator, and her company.)*

Some Tips on using Parentheses

● When parenthesised matter is inserted where there is a punctuation mark in a sentence, place the punctuation *after* the parenthesis:

The High Street (in Doncaster), Mrs May said, was typical of its kind.

● Don't place a dash before a bracketed parenthesis.

● If question marks or exclamation marks belong to the parenthesised matter, they should go *inside* the final bracket; if they relate to the main sentence they are placed *outside*:

Will you call Lucy this afternoon (or this evening if you are busy or away from your desk)?

Peter arrived home last night in a particularly happy frame of mind (and you know what I mean by happy!).

Square Brackets

Square brackets are not angular forms of round brackets; their function is entirely different from that of parentheses. Words enclosed within square brackets are not usually intended to be part of a sentence, but as an editorial or authorial interjection:

> *It was a matter of opinion that if offered the position, he [Professor Brandmeyer] would most likely refuse it on moral grounds.*

That sentence came at the end of a very long paragraph; the professor's name had been mentioned at the beginning, but other names and much discussion followed so that the late reference to *he* was in danger of being misunderstood. The editor therefore inserted the name [Professor Brandmeyer] in square brackets to remind readers who *he* was, and also to indicate that the intervention was the editor's and not the author's.

One of the most common uses of square brackets is to enclose the adverb *sic* (from the Latin *sicut*, meaning 'just as') to indicate that incorrect or doubtful matter is quoted exactly from the original:

> *Pink and yellow concubines [sic] climbed in great profusion up the trellis.*
> *The dog ran up to the car, whelping [sic] loudly and incessantly.*
> *Miss Patricia Wall Wall [sic] with her fiance Mr Gerald Kleeman.*

The last example was a caption under a photograph of the newly engaged couple; *The Times* wanted to make sure that readers understood that 'Wall Wall' really was the young lady's surname and not a misprint.

Square brackets are also used to supply or infer missing words:

> *Mrs Laverty insisted [that the] Council should note her objection in the official minutes.*

and to include parenthesised matter already in parenthesis:

> *Leonard's work has come in for censure and has been described as 'sloppy' (notably by G R Hooke in 'Amazonian Flora' [Phoenix Press, Boston, 1991] among others) and 'deplorably unreliable'.*

Brace brackets {brace brackets} and **angle brackets** <angle brackets> are used only in specialist texts, mathematics, tabulations and technical works.

A Dash to the Rescue

The dash is a much maligned mark. Newspaper style guides get quite stroppy on the subject. 'Dashes are a bad habit,' intones one, 'often used to pursue a line of thought that the writer cannot be bothered to construct in some other way.' Many grammar purists decry the substitution of the dash for the colon and pairs of dashes for parenthesising commas.

It is certainly true that dashes can be overused and misused. The Fowler brothers, in *The King's English*, quote a passage from Laurence Sterne's *Tristram Shandy* calculated to drive any reader up the wall:

> – Observe, I determine nothing upon this. – My way is ever to point out to the curious, different tracts of investigation, to come at the first springs of the events I tell:– not with a pedantic fescue, – or in the decisive manner of Tacitus, who outwits himself and his reader; – but with the officious humility . . . .

Sterne may be excused on the grounds that punctuation marks were only a couple of hundred years old when he wrote that and he was perhaps still a little uncertain of their functions, but there can be no excuse for the following over-dashed passage in an issue of *The Spectator* from our own age:

*There are also a great number of people – many of them not
in the least tainted by militarism – who go further and who
feel that a man in order to be a complete man – that is, one
capable of protecting his life, his country, and his civil and
political rights – should acquire as a boy and youth the
elements of military training – that is, should be given a
physical training . . .*

There will always be those who'll give a mark a bad name,
but in the last decade or two the dash has attracted a growing
band of defenders. 'It's the most exciting and dramatic
punctuation mark of them all,' claims one authority. Others admire
its flexibility and disdain for rules. The dash is a bit of a larrikin
and a lot of fun in the often po-faced world of punctuation.

One of its defenders is the formidable Eric Partridge (and
he is not alone; the Fowlers wrote a 15-page dissertation on the
mark) who, in a bold exposition in his *Usage and Abusage*,
pronounces full grammatical health on all these versions of the
same statement:

BRACKETS   *He was (God forgive him!) a scoundrel.*

COMMAS   *He was, God forgive him!, a scoundrel.*

SEMICOLONS   *He was; God forgive him!; a scoundrel.*

COLONS   *He was: God forgive him!: a scoundrel.*

Partridge did, however, have the grace to admit some
discomfort with the comma, semicolon and colon versions, before
commending the version with dashes:

DASHES   *He was – God forgive him! – a scoundrel.*

89

It doesn't take too much grammatical nous to see that the statement using dashes is the strongest, most fittingly dramatic and least fussy of them all.

So while the dash has versatility (two dashes can *interrupt* a sentence – as they are doing now – while one can *extend* a sentence – like this) and grammatical respectability, it can also be a trap. Too many dashes can lead to writing that jars and irritates – as in the *Spectator* example – both visually and mentally. If one were to impose rules about dashes they might look like this:

- Don't use dashes in adjoining sentences (as above).

- Restrict their use to a pair per page.

- Try not to use the dash as an all-purpose punctuation mark.

● **Dashes for Parenthesising.**

The earlier example –

> *He was – God forgive him! – a scoundrel.*

is a good instance of a pair of dashes used to parenthesise a statement, and this usage is growing by the day. You could take just about any example of parenthesising brackets and substitute dashes, and today few would object. The following sentence could be constructed using brackets, but what's wrong with dashes?

> *The dogs are so passive – they are virtually impossible to goad or excite – that the breed makes an ideal children's pet.*

While few writers forget to pair off brackets, many fail to add the second dash, using a comma in its place. Here's the grammar authority G V Carey, from his book *Mind The Stop* (1939):

> *No wonder that in some matters the dash has fallen into disrepute, but I still maintain that, if kept in its place – and I make one here for luck, it's a very useful stop.*

Unfortunately Mr Carey's luck ran out in that sentence because he forgot to complete his parenthesis with a second dash between *luck* and *it*, where he has incorrectly and inconsistently placed a comma. It's a lesson to us all – not to be slapdash with the dash!

The Versatile Dash

Observant readers will have noticed that dashes aren't always the same length. That's because there are two sorts of dashes, their lengths based on the *em*, the basic printers' measurement. The standard dash – is one em in length and is called the **em dash**. The other kind is called the **en dash** - and is exactly half the length of the em, and, incidentally, twice the length of the hyphen. The en dash is predominantly a typographic device for specific usages: *Vols I-XII; 1914-1918 War; London-Paris flight; pages 21-25; June-July; 4.00-6.00pm*, etc. So much for technicalities; all further discussion is confined to the em dash.

Here are some examples where the dash can be used legitimately, appropriately, and – yes – even elegantly. The first of these is perhaps also the most common of usages: substituting for colons.

LINKING DEVICE

Mrs Sims had four daughters – Poppy, Iris, Pansy and Petal.

On that particular evening, Malcolm had one consuming passion – to drink the place dry.

AS A PAUSE

Everyone expected the speaker to be controversial – but not to the extent of swearing at the chairwoman and falling off the stage.

ADDING EMPHASIS

There is nothing – absolutely nothing – that will make me change my mind about Harry.

NOTING AN EXCEPTION

A straight line is the shortest distance between two points – when you're sober.

INDICATING DISRUPTION AND INTERRUPTION

'There will be, of course, er – a small charge, but if you, er – '

'Hang on – you never said anything about a charge – not a word – there's no way –'

INDICATING HESITATION

'I'm sorry. It was – you know – '
'Well – what – ?'

SEPARATING LISTS

She assembled all the ingredients – flour, sugar, eggs, salt, lard and raisins – and started on the pudding.

AFTERTHOUGHT

They babbled on, delighted at sighting the rare parakeet – I didn't see so much as a feather.

SIGNALLING A SURPRISE

Then the adhesive gave way, the beard came adrift, and Santa Claus was revealed as – Aunt Mildred!

David Marquand is one of those rare commodities in British politics – an intellectual.

The latter example demonstrates one of the most creative usages of the dash – that of signalling a surprise ahead or, in the words of H W Fowler, 'inviting the reader to pause and collect his forces against the shock of an unexpected word that is to close the sentence.' Lord Byron was particularly adept at this:

There is a tide in the affairs of women which, taken at the flood, leads – God knows where.
He learned the arts of riding, fencing, gunnery and how to scale a fortress – or a nunnery.

The Dash in Sentence Construction

For some examples of the use of the dash by a master of the language, here are some excerpts from Shiva Naipaul's *Love and Death in a Hot Country*. First, see how he chooses to use a dash to introduce the subjects, and then a colon to set off a conclusion:

Everything seemed more dramatic than ever – Aubrey, the woman he called his wife, himself, the hot square of garden: shadows whose actions and words he did not fully understand.

Secondly, he prefers dashes to parenthesise, rather than commas:

Dina had no idea what – if anything – was expected of her.

And, again, dashes substitute for colons:

Imagine a family – a family, if you wish, like my own.

Finally, here's a long parenthetical passage that few writers would want to attempt. But see how, after the closing dash, Naipaul cleverly repeats his opening phrase *the surprising thing*, so that the reader, whose attention might have drifted, is smartly reunited with the main sentence:

*The surprising thing about the imminent abandonment
of the Constitution – that lengthy charter so top-heavy
with ringing preambles, so glutinously coated with abstract
principles of right and justice and obligation, so ribboned
with guarantees to minorities and special interests, so
honeycombed with promises of life and liberty and happiness
for all, so stiff with austere legalism, so sweetened with the
codes of civility, that Constitution painstakingly fabricated
and assembled over several weeks in panelled, chandeliered
halls and flourished in triumph at the climax – the surprising
thing was not that it was about to be unceremoniously tossed
out of the window but that it had taken such a comparatively
long time for that to happen.*

A Dashed Quotation Quiz

The original quotations all contained dashes, but have been repunctuated. Can you correctly reinstate the dashes?

1. *No! No! Sentence first, verdict afterwards.*
   – Lewis Carroll

2. *The English country gentleman – galloping after a fox: the unspeakable in full pursuit of the uneatable. –* Oscar Wilde

3. *Every woman should marry. And no man. –* Disraeli

4. *Familiarity breeds contempt . . . and children.*
   – Mark Twain

5. *Don't clap too hard; it's an old building.*
   – John Osborne

6. *Sweet is revenge, especially to women.*
   – Lord Byron

Answers: *1. first – verdict 2. fox – the 3. marry – and 4. contempt – and 5. hard – it's 6. revenge – especially.*

Hassles with Hyphens

Did you ever see a window dressing? A worm eaten, or a cut throat? Witnessed a U turn? Or have you heard a name calling? Obviously not, but just to make sure nobody is hoodwinked we tend to hyphenate such compound words:

window-dressing; worm-eaten; cut-throat; U-turn; name-calling

But not always. Among punctuation marks the hyphen is the most liable to variant usage, illogical exceptions and change. To those who like this sort of situation, hyphens are the splice of life.

We've dealt with dashes and know that they are used, in various ways, to help us *construct sentences*. The hyphen helps us to *construct words* to clarify meaning. At least that's what they set out to do.

Here are two similar newspaper headlines:

MAN EATING TIGER SEEN NEAR MOTORWAY.

MAN-EATING TIGER SEEN NEAR MOTORWAY.

The first headline suggests that a hungry gourmet has decided to barbecue some choice jungle beast near a motorway, while the second could prove fatal should you be carelessly wandering along the hard shoulder. A hyphen has made all the difference.

In the same vein, *a little used car* (say a Mini) is not in the same league as *a little-used car* (say a 6-litre Rolls-Royce with only 3,000 miles on the clock). Nor is a *small businessman* necessarily a *small-businessman*, or a *French polisher* a *French-polisher*. To quote a notorious example, a consignment of *superfluous hair-remover* could have a devastating effect on someone looking for the benefits of *superfluous-hair remover*. So beware!

97

The Evolutionary Hyphen

Hyphens are used to join, temporarily or permanently, two or more associated words. Sometimes this is done to create a useful compound word to describe something for which no word exists *(double-cross, off-putting, knock-kneed)*. Sometimes it is done to remove potential confusion *(tie-break; stick-up, re-cover)*, or to act as a guide to pronunciation *(get-at-able, co-respondent)*.

One of the most interesting qualities of the hyphen is that, having done its job, it is often discarded and – *presto!* – a new word is born, unencumbered by punctuation. This process can take half a century or a decade. If you had lived in the 1950s you would have read words such as *motor-car, tax-payer* and *man-power*. Today, as we know, they are single words without hyphens. And *today* itself was *to-day* in the early 20th century; *tomorrow* was *to-morrow* and *yesterday* was *yester-day*.

This evolutionary process, however, is not consistent; some hyphenated compounds make it to respectability and some don't:

SEPARATE WORDS	HYPHENATED COMPOUND	UNIFIED COMPOUND
son in law	*son-in-law*	(unlikely)
book seller	*book-seller*	*bookseller*
book keeper	*book-keeper*	(unlikely)
life like	*life-like*	*lifelike*

Sometimes the transition can be dated with great accuracy. In 1935 the American mystery novelist Raymond Chandler coined the term *cover-up*. It lost its hyphen in the early 1970s to become the very useful word *coverup*, although you may still find the hyphenated version lingering in some dictionaries. The hyphenated compound *hand-operated* was introduced in 1936 and *child-proof* saw first light of day in 1956 to join a confused family: *child-bearing* (hyphenated); *child benefit, child labour, child's play, child minder* (all two words) and *childbed, childbirth, childhood* and *childlike* (unified words). But turn your back for a few moments and you may find that some of the family have shed their hyphens while others have acquired them.

Obviously, when it comes to hyphens, inconsistencies abound. Even as late as the 1960s it was the style of many institutions and publications in the UK for street names to be hyphenated: *Oxford-street, Parliament-street, Drury-lane, Harper-road*. And half a century ago it was not uncommon to see *publichouse* in print and on signs. Since then the single word has taken a reverse trip and is now *public house*, or *pub* for short. But that's a rare case; for most hyphenated compounds the goal is to become a 'proper' word. Here are just a few of thousands of words that began life as two or more words linked by hyphens:

> *anticlimax, bloodyminded, businesslike, contradict,*
> *contraflow, earring, hindquarters, lampshade, lifestyle,*
> *nightgown, nowadays, phoenixlike, postgraduate,*
> *posthumous, predeceased, predecessor, prehistoric, seaside,*
> *washbowl.*

Then there are those hyphenated partners never destined to marry because of 'letter collision' which is visually disconcerting: *shell-like* (not *shelllike*); *semi-illiterate* (not *semiilliterate*); *de-ice* (not *deice*); *co-wrote* (not *cowrote*) – although we accept such unhyphenated pairs of spectacles as *cooperative* and *coordination*.

99

Compound Engagements, Marriages and Divorces

As we have seen, there are pairs of words that have a hyphenated romance, become engaged, and sometimes marry. There are others that never make the commitment although they're often seen together, even live together, and still others – a minority – that separate or become divorced. Just like life, there's a lot of promiscuity among compound words. But is there a recognisable *pattern* in this teeming sub-world of compounding?

Well, yes, despite the exceptions and inconsistencies, there is. The vast majority of compound words are constructed from a headword and a prefix (*ex-sailor*, **semi**-*detached*, **anti**-*hero*); a headword and a suffix (*shoot-**out***, *phone-**in***, *crack-**down***) or with two or more different parts of speech (two nouns = **book-end**; noun and verb = **joy-ride**; two verbs = **dry-clean**, etc). Most of these compounds follow group patterns, some being hyphenated and some not, as you will see, although there will be the inevitable rebels. Here's a guide to the more common problematical compound words.

Compounds with Prefixes

- **all-** Usually hyphenated: *all-American, all-important, all-round, all-out, all-powerful, all-sorts, all-star, all-time, all-inclusive.* **Exceptions:** *all clear, all in, all fours, all right, all square, allspice, All Blacks.*

- **ante-** Invariably a single word: *antecedent, antechamber, antedate, antediluvian, antenatal, anteroom.*

- **anti-** Always a single word; hyphenated only to avoid ambiguity: *antibiotic, anticlimax, anticlockwise, anticyclone, antifreeze, antimacassar, antislavery.* **Exceptions:** *anti-aircraft, anti-American, anti-hero, anti-personnel, anti-icer.*

- **back-** Generally one word: *backache, backbone, backdrop, background, backstroke, backwater.* **Exceptions:** *back burner, back-pedal, back seat, back up.*

- **bi-** Typically one word: *biannual, biennial, bifocal, bilateral, bilingual, bisexual, biweekly.* **Exceptions:** *bi-weekly* and *bi-monthly* are also commonly seen.

- **by-** Careful – a mixed bag: *by and by, by and large, bye-bye, by-election, bylaw, bypass, by-product, bystander, bygone, bypass, byword.*

- **co-** Always a single word but hyphenated when meaning may be unclear. **Exceptions:** *co-opt, co-respondent, co-author, co-driver, co-op, co-star.*

- **contra-** Always one word: *contradistinction, contrapuntal.*

- **cross-** Usually hyphenated: *cross-breed, cross-country, cross-eyed, cross-legged.* **Exceptions:** *crossbar, crossbow, crosscut, crossover, crossroad, cross section, crosswind, crossword.*

- **de-** Always a single word and only hyphenated where 'letter collision' occurs: *de-ice, de-emphasise, de-escalate.*

- **die-** Single word. **Exceptions:** *die-cast, die-cut, die-hard, die down.*

- **ex-** Most words beginning with the prefix *ex-* are single words (*except, excise, exclamation, existential,* etc) but there are two important exceptions: (1) where the meaning is 'formerly' or the word conveys a sense of exclusion, it is hyphenated, and (2) terms derived from Latin have the *ex* separate, with no hyphen. **Exceptions (1):** *ex-husband, ex-convict, ex-serviceman, ex-colleague, ex-president, ex-Foreign Secretary, ex-directory;* **(2):** *ex dividend, ex gratia, ex libris, ex officio, ex parte.* Also *ex works.*

- **extra-** Most dictionaries now drop the hyphen (*extracurricular, extramarital, extrasensory*) but some words look clearer and cleaner with one: *extra-illustrated, extra-terrestrial.*

- **far-** Usually hyphenated: *far-fetched, far-flung, far-off, far-reaching, far-seeing, far-sighted.* **Exceptions:** *far cry, Far East.*

- **foot-** Always a single word. **Exceptions:** *foot-and-mouth disease, foot brake, foot-candle, foot-pound.*

- **full-** Usually hyphenated: *full-frontal, full-length, full-scale.* **Exceptions:** *full board, full house, full moon, full time, full stop, full toss, fullback.*

- **get-** Two separate words: *get away, get by, get off, get on, get up.* **Exceptions:** *getaway, get-at-able, get-together, get-up-and-go.*

- **go-** Either two words (*go ahead, go on, go under*) or hyphenated: *go-by, go-kart, go-getter, go-go, go-slow.* **Exceptions:** *goer.*

- **half-** Mostly hyphenated: *half-cocked, half-length, half-time.*
  Exceptions: *halfback, half board, half holiday, half measure, half term, halftone, halfway.*

- **hard-** Very little uniformity here! Nouns are mostly single words: *hardback, hardboard, hardcore, hardship, hardtop.* Some nouns, however, are two separate words: *hard copy, hard court, hard hat, hard labour, hard line.* Where the prefix forms an adjective the word is hyphenated: *hard-bitten, hard-edged, hard-headed, hard-hitting, hard-nosed, hard-pressed, hard-working.*

- **in-** Single words except when the *in-* prefix is specifically used to indicate belonging or 'within', when the word is hyphenated *(in-built, in-crowd, in-depth, in-house, in-law)* or derives from Latin: *in situ, in utero, in vitro.* **Exception:** *inpatient.*

- **lay-** Two words: *lay days, lay off, lay over.* **Exceptions:** *layabout, lay-by, layman, laywoman, layout.*

- **neo-** The trend is to drop the traditional hyphen: *neoclassical, neocolonial, neorealism.* **Exceptions:** *Neo-Darwinism, neo-Nazism, neo-orthodoxy.*

- **no-** Hyphenated: *no-claim bonus, no-good, no-show, no-man's-land, no-nonsense, no-ball.* **Exceptions:** *nobody, nowhere.*

- **non-** Traditionally hyphenated but there's a trend now to drop the hyphen: *nondelivery, nondrip, nondrinker, nonexistent, nonirritant, nonstop.* **Exceptions:** *non-navigable, non-negotiable, non-U, non-striker, non sequitur.*

- **off-**   Usually hyphenated: *off-centre, off-licence, off-load, off-peak, off-white, off-putting, off-Broadway.*
  Exceptions: *offbeat, offcut, offhand, off key, off limits, off season, offshoot, offside, offstage.*

- **on-**   Usually a single word: *oncoming, ongoing, onlooker, onset, onside.* **Exceptions:** *on-cost, on-drive, on-off, on key, on line.*

- **out-**   Usually one word: *outbuilding, outcry, outlying, outpatient.* **Exceptions:** *out-and-out, out-of-doors.*

- **over-**   Overwhelmingly one word: *overact, overcharge, overhear, overstate.* **Exception:** *over-the-counter.*

- **per-**   Nearly always one word. The only exceptions are Latin terms: *per annum, per cent, per se.*

- **pre-**   Invariably one word: *preconceive, prefabricate, preoccupy, preview.* **Exceptions:** *pre-Gothic, pre-Renaissance,* and similarly with other proper nouns.

- **pro-**   Usually hyphenated when the meaning of the prefix is 'in favour or in support of': *pro-British, pro-European,* etc. But the trend is to drop the hyphen when it precedes a common noun: *probusiness, proreform.*

- **quasi-**   Always hyphenated: *quasi-official, quasi-judicial,* etc.

- **re-**   Single word except when 'letter collision' occurs (*re-edit, re-embark, re-engage, re-enact, re-enter, re-establish*) or when there is confusion over meaning: *re-count, re-cover, re-create, re-entry, re-form, re-lay, re-present, re-serve.*

- **self-** Invariably hyphenated: *self-assured, self-contained, self-denial, self-evident, self-respect.* **Exception:** *selfsame.*

- **semi-** Single word except when 'letter collision' occurs: *semi-industrial, semi-illiterate, semi-intoxicated, semi-invalid.*

- **set-** Usually two words: *set off, set piece, set square, set up, set upon.* **Exception:** *set-aside* (EC farm subsidy scheme).

- **sub-** Usually one word: *subcontinent, subcontractor, subheading.* **Exceptions:** *sub-branch, sub-basement, sub-post office, sub-machine gun.*

- **super-** Always one word: *superannuated, superego, supermarket.*

- **trans-** Always one word: *transcendental, transferable, transformer.*

- **tri-** Always one word: *triangulate, trilateral, tristate.*

- **un-** Always one word: *unfulfilled, unheeded, uninvitingly.*

- **up-** Usually one word: *upbeat, upheaval, upmost, upriver, upstage.* **Exceptions:** *up-anchor, up-and-coming, up-market, up-to-date.*

- **vice-** When the prefix denotes a substitute the noun is usually hyphenated: *vice-chairman, vice-chancellor, vice-captain.* **Exceptions:** *vice admiral, viceregal, viceroy, vice president* (but *vice-presidency*).

Compounds with Suffixes

- **-all**   Usually hyphenated: *be-all, catch-all.*
  Exception: *holdall.*

- **-away**   The trend is to drop the traditional hyphen: *faraway, giveaway, breakaway.*

- **-back**   Invariably one word: *cutback, flashback, playback, throwback.*

- **-by**   One word: *whereby, standby, hereby.* **Exception:** *go-by.*

- **-down**   Depending on the part of speech the words are playing, a variable group: the verb *back down* becomes *backdown* as a noun; *put down* as a verb becomes a *put-down*, the noun; the noun *breakdown* becomes *broken-down* as an adjective. Some single-word nouns include *meltdown, crackdown, showdown, slowdown,* while *close-down, sit-down* and *run-down* are usually hyphenated.

- **-fold**   Always single word: *twofold, hundredfold.*

- **-free**   Usually hyphenated: *fat-free, sugar-free, scot-free.*

- **-in**   Usually hyphenated: *built-in, drive-in, sit-in, trade-in.*

- **-less**   Always single word: *defenceless, lifeless, regardless.*

- **-like**   Single word except when 'letter collision' occurs: *owl-like, shell-like.*

- **-off**   Traditionally hyphenated *(lay-off, rip-off, turn-off, well-off, write-off)* but there is a trend to drop the hyphen: *breakoff, brushoff, kickoff, liftoff.*

- **-on**   Invariably hyphenated: *come-on, follow-on, goings-on, knock-on, put-on, roll-on / roll-off, slip-on, try-on.*

- **-out**   Traditionally hyphenated but succumbing to the trend of dropping the hyphen: *blackout, checkout, hideout, lookout, tryout, wipeout.*

- **-over**   Usually single word: *pushover, takeover, walkover.*

- **-up**   Usually hyphenated: *blow-up, call-up, cover-up, foul-up, make-up, mark-up, press-up, stand-up* (adj).
               Exception: *hang up.*

Other Compounds

Apart from compound words formed by headwords with prefixes and suffixes, there are thousands of other words in which various parts of speech have been combined:

NOUN + VERB	*ham-fisted, hand-operated*
ADJECTIVE + NOUN	*blue-pencil, loose-leaf, long-grain, open-air*
ADJECTIVE + ADJECTIVE	*old-fashioned, short-sighted, cold-blooded*

. . . and so on. Although many of these compounds stick to rules just as many have abandoned them, so it is pointless to search for helpful patterns. Overleaf, you'll find a hotchpotch of words generally accepted as requiring hyphens at the time of publication:

A Hotchpotch of Hyphens

accident-prone, acid-free, aide-de-camp, aide-mémoire, anti-abortion, après-ski, argy-bargy, attorney-at-law, Attorney-General, avant-garde, awe-inspiring.

baby-boomer, back-seat driver, ball-and-socket joint, bas-relief, big-bang theory, bird-brain, bird's-eye view, bleary-eyed, bloody-minded, blow-dry, bone-dry, bone-shaking, boogie-woogie, book-keeping, book-keeper, brain-teaser, bric-a-brac, bright-eyed and bushy-tailed, bring-and-buy, brother-in-law, bull's-eye, by-product.

call-up, can-opener, cast-offs, catch-as-catch-can, cat-o'-nine-tails, chef-d'oeuvre, clear-eyed, Coca-Cola, cock-a-doodle-do, cock-and-bull story, co-driver, cold-blooded, cold-hearted, come-hither, co-op, co-worker, counter-revolution, crash-landing, crease-resistant, Creutzfeldt-Jakob disease, cross-index, cul-de-sac, custom-built, cut-throat.

daddy-longlegs, daughter-in-law, deaf-and-dumb, deep-sea fishing, devil-may-care, devils-on-horseback, dewy-eyed, ding-dong, do-it-yourself, door-to-door, double-cross, double-dealing, double-park, Dow-Jones, down-and-out, dry-stone wall, dyed-in-the-wool.

eagle-eyed, ear-splitting, eau-de-Cologne, egg-and-spoon race, empty-handed, Entre-Deux-Mers, even-tempered, evil-minded, eye-opener.

face-lift, *face-saving, fact-finding, fancy-free, far-seeing, father-in-law, fault-finding, felt-tip pen, fifty-fifty, first-day cover, first-hand, five-o'clock shadow, five-star hotel, flag-waving, fleur-de-lis, fly-by-night, follow-my-leader, foot-and-mouth disease, force-feed, forget-me-not, fortune-teller, foul-mouthed, four-letter-word,* fractions *(three-quarters, one-twentieth,* etc), *free-for-all, French-polish, full-blown, full-bodied.*

gap-toothed, *gender-bender, get-at-able, get-together, give-and-take, glow-worm, glue-sniffing, go-go dancer, gold-digger, gold-plate* (**verb**), *good-for-nothing, good-humoured, good-looking, good-natured, good-time girl, grass-roots, great-aunt/niece/nephew, grief-stricken, grown-ups, G-string.*

habit-forming, *hag-ridden, hail-fellow-well-met, hair-raising, hair's-breadth, half-a-crown, half-and-half, half-breed* (virtually all words prefixed with half- are hyphenated, as noted), *hand-held, hand-me-downs, hand-out, hand-pick, hands-off, hand-to-hand, hand-to-mouth, hanger-on, hanky-panky, happy-go-lucky, hard-bitten, hard-edged, hard-headed, hard-hitting, hard-nosed, hard-pressed, hard-sell, hard-wearing, head-on collision, heart-to-heart, heart-searching, heart-warming, heave-ho, heaven-sent, heavy-duty, heavy-handed, helter-skelter, he-man, hide-and-seek, hi-fi, higgledy-piggledy, high-class, high-flown, high-handed, high-spirited, high-tech/level/minded/octane/powered/rise/risk/speed/tension, hip-hop, hit-and-run, hocus-pocus, home-grown, home-made, horror-stricken, hot-air balloon, hot-dog stand, hot-water bottle, hound's-tooth check, house-proud, Hula-Hoop, hunky-dory, hurdy-gurdy, hurly-burly.*

ice-cream soda/cone (but *ice cream*), *ill-advised/assorted/behaved/bred/considered/disposed/fated/mannered/natured/starred/timed/treated, in-built, in-house.*

jack-in-the-box, jack-o'-lantern, Jack-the-lad, jiggery-pokery, Johnny-come-lately, jumped-up, jump-start.

kick-start, king-size, kiss-and-tell, knee-deep/high/length, knees-up, knick-knack, knife-point, knock-for-knock, knock-kneed, knock-on, knuckle-duster.

labour-intensive, labour-saving, lady-in-waiting, laid-back, laissez-faire, lamb's-wool jumper, land-holder, Land-Rover, large-scale, last-ditch, last-gasp, Latter-day Saint, lean-to, left-handed, lèse-majesté, level-headed, lickety-spit, life-size, life-support, light-headed, light-sensitive, like-minded, lily-white, line-up, lived-in, long-distance runner/phone call, long-drawn-out, long-standing, long-suffering, long-term memory, long-winded, look-see, loose-limbed, lop-eared, low-key, low-water mark, lying-in.

major-domo, make-believe, make-up, mal-de-mer, man-eater, mange-tout, man-o'-war, man-to-man, mark-up, mass-market (*adj, vb*), mealy-mouthed, mezzo-soprano, middle-aged, mind-boggling, mind-blowing, mind-reader, mind-set, mix-up, morning-after feeling, mother-in-law, mother-of-pearl, mouth-to-mouth, multiple-choice, muu-muu.

name-calling, name-dropping, near-sighted, ne'er-do-well, never-ending, never-never, night-light, nit-picking, no-claim bonus, no-go area, no-show, no-hoper, non-starter, nuclear-free zone.

off-Broadway, off-centre, off-peak, off-putting, off-the-wall, old-fashioned, old-time dancing, O-level, one-night-stand, one-parent family, one-piece, one-to-one, one-way ticket, out-of-doors.

Pan-American, pari-mutuel, passe-partout, passer-by, pay-as-you-go, penny-wise, pound-foolish, penny-pinching, pent-up (*adj*), pied-a-terre, pile-driver, Ping-Pong, pitch-and-toss, pitter-patter, place-name, point-blank, point-to-point, pooh-pooh, pooper-scooper, pop-up, post-natal, *post-paid, pre-eminent, pre-empt, pre-natal, pressure-cook, price-fixing, pro-choice, punch-drunk, purpose-built, push-start.*

quarter-hour, *quarter-miler, Queen-Anne* (style), *quick-change, quick-tempered, quick-witted.*

rake-off, *razor-cut, ready-mix, rear-view mirror, red-blooded/ handed/headed, red-letter day, reel-to-reel, right-handed/minded/thinking, rip-roaring, Rolls-Royce, roly-poly, root-canal treatment, rose-coloured, run-of-the-mill, rye-grass.*

sabre-rattling, *St Martin-in-the-Fields, Saint-Saens, sang-froid, savoir-faire, sawn-off, scot-free, second-guess, self-abuse* (nearly all words with the *self-* prefix are hyphenated), *set-aside, seven-year itch, sex-starved, sharp-eyed, shirt-tail, short-changed, short-lived, short-staffed, sickle-cell anaemia, side-splitting, silver-gilt, silver-tongued, simon-pure, single-lens reflex, sit-down strike, six-gun/shooter, skin-deep, smarty-pants, smooth-tongued, so-called, soft-boiled egg, softly-softly, soft-shoe shuffle, son-in-law, space-bar, spick-and-span, spin-off, standard-bearer, stick-up, stone-cold, stone-deaf, straight-from-the-shoulder, strait-laced, strong-arm, sun-dried, surface-to-air missile, sweet-and-sour, sweet-talk, swing-wing, swollen-headed.*

tailor-made, *tam-o'-shanter, tax-deductable/exempt/free, terror-stricken, test-drive (**vb**), test-tube baby, tête-à-tête, thick-skinned, think-tank, thin-skinned, third-rate, three-dimensional, three-piece, three-ply, three-ring circus, three-wheeler, tic-tac-toe, tip-off, toad-in-the-hole, ton-up, top-flight, touch-type, trade-off, trap-door spider, travel-sickness, treasure-trove, turbo-electric, tut-tut, tutti-frutti, twin-tub, two faced/handed/seater/sided/step/tone, two-way mirror.*

U-bend, *U-boat, ultra-violet* (but often *ultraviolet*), *up-and-coming, up-market, upside-down cake, upsy-daisy, up-to-date, U-turn.*

value-added tax, vice-presidential, V-day, vis-a-vis, VJ-Day, voice-over, vol-au-vent, volte-face.

walk-on part, walkie-talkie, wall-to-wall, warm-hearted, wash-and-wear, washing-up, watch-glass, weak-willed, weather-beaten, well-appointed (words with the *well-* prefix are always hyphenated), well-to-do, whistle-blower, white-hot, white-knuckle ride, whole-wheat, wide-awake, wide-angle lens, will-o'-the-wisp, willy-willy, wind-borne, window-dresser, window-shopping, wishy-washy, witch-hunt, work-in-progress, world-beater/class/weary, worm-eaten, would-be, wrong-footed, wrong-headed, wych-elm.

X-chromosome, X-ray (or x-ray).

Y-chromosome, yellow-bellied, year-round, yo-heave-ho, yo-ho-ho.

zero-rated.

Other Functions of the Hyphen

One of the most useful functions of the hyphen is probably the one we notice least: that of syllabification or **syllabication** (syl-lab-i-ca-tion) – the hyphen's role in enabling us to split words at the end of lines. When this is done according to the logic of word construction the reader's eye travels from one line to the next without interruption or effort. But it is apparent that some modern typesetting software follows no such rules and words are likely to be divided on rather more *laissez-faire* principles, giving rise to such unlikely compounds as *fig-urine, the-ories, leg-end, should-er, condom-inium, physiothe-rapists, hor-semen, screwd-river, mans-laughter* and so on. Fortunately most typesetting today is automatically justified (aligned to the left and right) and whole books can be printed without resorting to wordbreaks at all.

Hyphens are essential for separating certain groups of words or names *(The Conservative-Liberal Alliance; The Paris-Washington Accord)* and to make sense of double double-barrel surnames where the central dividing hyphen is more a 'short' dash: *The event of the county season was the Hywell-Jones–Craig-Thomas wedding in May.* Remember, too, that many English place-names are traditionally hyphenated:

Burton-on-Trent, Newcastle-upon-Tyne, Stow-on-the-Wold, Weston-super-Mare.

Hyphens are also useful for creating special effects:

'Blimey, it's c-c-c-cold in here!'

'I repeat, my name is Smyth – S-M-Y-T-H – not Smith!'

'I'm b-b-bloody sick of this n-n-nonsense!' he spluttered.

Occasionally you may need to use what is called the **suspensive hyphen** to avoid repetition:

Between Monday and Thursday there were two-, four-, seven- and five-inch snowfalls.

But watch this usage warily; it's not pretty. Better to try to reconstruct the sentence:

Four snowfalls were recorded between Monday and Thursday, of two, four, seven and five inches.

If this chapter on hyphens has seemed a touch heavy-handed you might consider the words of writer and grammatical realist Keith Waterhouse: 'If you write *second-hand* and *car salesman,* should you write *second-hand-car salesman*, which is fussy, or *second-hand car salesman*, which suggests that the salesman is second-hand? Fruitless hours can be spent pondering such questions. It is usually better to leave all the hyphens out than allow them to pile up.'

An Inadequacy of Hyphens

Keith Waterhouse's thoughts apart, the following passage suffers from a dearth of hyphens. Can you supply them?

We were headed cross country for Stratford on Avon, mother in law in the rear and running late for the seven o'clock curtain. It was an ill fated, accident prone journey, with an hour spent on a lay by with a broken down three wheeler – ten year old cars aren't always a hundred per cent reliable – gathering forget me nots in knee high rye grass and wondering, bleary eyed, if we would ever get to the theatre.

(Suggested punctuation below)

An Inadequacy of Hyphens: Suggested Punctuation

*We were headed **cross-country** for **Stratford-on-Avon**, **mother-in-law** in the rear and running late for the **seven-o'clock** curtain. It was an **ill-fated**, **accident-prone** journey, with an hour spent on a **lay-by** with a **broken-down three-wheeler** – **ten-year-old** cars aren't always a hundred per cent reliable – gathering **forget-me-nots** in **knee-high rye-grass** and wondering, **bleary-eyed**, if we would ever get to the theatre.*

114

Symbols of Meaning

Any Questions?
The Question Mark

So far we've dealt with units of space, separation and connection. Now we enter new punctuation territory: the rest of our marks are symbols of expression and meaning.

The question mark and exclamation mark share a common ancestry: both are developments of the full stop. The exclamation mark consists of a hanging stroke pointing emphatically to the stop below it to make the reader screech to a halt. The question mark has a squiggle atop the stop, not unlike a '*q*' (for *query*?), and its purpose is to warn the reader that the preceding word or statement is interrogative, or of doubtful validity. Furthermore, they are all prone to stray into each other's territory:

You're going.　　　　is not the same as　　　　*You're going?*

You're going?　　　　is not the same as　　　　*You're going!*

Same words, but the three different symbols enable us to express three shades of meaning:

● *You're going.*　=　"*James, I know you've got a bit of a cold, but not bad enough to stay home from school. You're going.*"

116

- *You're going?* = *"You're going? So soon? But you've just arrived."*

- *You're going!* = *"For the last time, James, whether you like it or not – you're going!"*

Undoubtedly the question mark is a simple but useful punctuation device, although there are those who, inadvertently or deliberately, avoid it. One of the latter is the American comic novelist J P Donleavy who, somewhere between writing *The Ginger Man* (1955) and *A Singular Man* (1964) decided to eschew the question mark altogether. Here's a typical passage, where the hero George Smith asks his secretary to look into his eyes:

'Just tell me what colour they are.'
'I think they're green, Mr Smith.'
'I mean the whites, what are they.'
'White. Mr Smith.'

'How white.'
'Just white, Mr Smith.'
'You don't think they're going grey.'
'No, Mr Smith.'
'Or brown.'
'No.'

Such a passage is attributed by critics to "Donleavy's idiosyncratic style" which aside from his refusal to employ question marks includes casually dropping other marks and ending sentences at odd places. To many readers, however, such mannerisms can be intensely irritating. Moreover, playing games with punctuation has its pitfalls; in Donleavy's case his no doubt frustrated editor found that in *A Singular Man* at least one question mark was necessary to avoid confusion. Here's the passage (Chapter 10):

> "We thought the guy was nuts. A friend of yours? We were going to call the cops but he was gone all of a sudden. Left an envelope. On the window sill of the office. Are you from the institution."

Direct and Indirect Questions

A sentence that asks a question directly requires a question mark, but a sentence that poses an *indirect question* does not:

DIRECT QUESTION   *'Are you going to the match?'*

INDIRECT QUESTION   *'I asked him if he was going to the match.'*

This looks fairly simple but sometimes an indirect question can be disguised. Here's a sub-headline from *The Sunday Times*:

A hundred years after Freud, 50 after the development of potent psychiatric drugs, have our ideas of psychiatric care really progressed, asks Dr Anthony Clare.

Not a question mark in sight! Why? Here's another example, from *The Times*:

Why should allegations that go unchallenged in America be the subject of legal action in Britain, asks Roy Greenslade.

Both sentences seem to be screaming for question marks – the first after *progressed*, the other after *Britain*. But if you study the sentences carefully you will see that both are just novel forms of indirect questions. Taking the second example, we could write it so that its indirect status is not the least in doubt:

Roy Greenslade asks why should allegations that go unchallenged in America be the subject of legal action in Britain.

Or in the form of a reported direct question:

Roy Greenslade asks, "Why should allegations that go unchallenged in America be the subject of legal action in Britain?"

Here's another perplexing example, this time carrying a question mark:

I wonder how many people will be homeless this Christmas?

Look closely and you'll see that this is an indirect question. So why is it followed by a question mark? This is because many writers fall into this error; the sentence should end with a full stop. Either that, or rewrite the sentence to include a direct question:

> *I wondered, "How many people will be homeless this Christmas?"*

One of the curious and confusing characteristics of the question mark is that you have to reach the end of the sentence to be certain that a question is being asked. This isn't a problem with short questions, but when you strike an interminably long question, it can be. Don't forget that, no matter how long your sentence is, if there is a direct question contained in it, a question mark is still required:

> *Is it not curious that Emile Zola's 'Lourdes', which within a year of publication sold over 200,000 copies, had critical acclaim poured over it like champagne and which provoked such a furore that it was instantly placed on the Vatican's Index of prohibited books, is not still widely read today?*

After reading that passage most of us would agree that there is a good case for placing the question mark at the beginning to signal to the reader that a question is coming, as they do in Spain.

Most of us, most of the time, use question marks at the most simplistic level. But for those who might wish to wield this mark with more panache, let's explore a little deeper into its usage. Here is the mark being used in several ways:

INTERROGATIVE	*Are you from Canada?*
DECLARATIVE	*Do you fully realise the trouble you're in?*
EXCLAMATORY	*Isn't this just fantastic?*
TAG QUESTION	*It's a great game, isn't it?*
REQUEST	*Would you let me know if either Monday or Tuesday next week would be suitable?*

The first of these is of course the common, simple question that a child quickly learns how to use. The second type isn't so simple; besides being a question it also carries strong overtones of frustration, curtness, even anger. The **exclamatory question**, appropriately named, could end with an exclamation mark and yet still remain a question. The **tag question** reinforces the first part of the sentence by seeking agreement from the person or persons being addressed; it is one of the most common conversational bonding devices. The **request question** is the most slippery of them all; for example, requests typically beginning with the question 'Would you . . . ' often finish with a full stop.

The 'Semi'-question

Would you be good enough to ensure that in future cars and other vehicles belonging to non-staff are parked outside the gates.

Well, what is it – a request or a question? It is in fact both, part question, part demand. A writer wishing to be polite or agreeable would add a question mark – but that would weaken the authority of the request. Where do you draw the line? Many writers are troubled by this weasel-like quality. Look at these examples – all questions – but all reasonably comfortable without a question mark:

> *I trust you're not going to give in so soon, John.*
>
> *I hope you're not calling me a liar.*
>
> *I wonder if I might borrow the car tomorrow.*

In these cases, the expressions of personal feeling – *I trust, I hope* and *I wonder* – tend to undermine the question content of the statements. If you wrote *You're not going to give in yet?* or *May I borrow the car tomorrow?* you'd unhesitatingly finish with question marks. But there are some questions that look quite strange with question marks:

> *How dare you?*   *How dare you!*

Here the expression is more an angry exclamation than a query, and a question mark would, in this and most similar cases, seem inappropriate. Usage of the question mark demands a little thought sometimes; if you can't work it out logically, perhaps your ear will guide you.

Other Questions about the Question Mark

Novel applications of the question mark are abhorred by some grammarians but there is no denying that they are useful:

> *The coins were thought to be from the reign of Emperor Tiberius (?130-86BC).*

Many of the students claimed that they owed their success in life to the loving care (?) of the college's headmaster and his wife.

The former is considered to be acceptable while the latter – the snide question mark to indicate doubt, cynicism or sarcasm – is frowned upon by the purists. The use is brilliantly economical but there are more elegant ways to convey our scepticism of suspect assertions. Take this example:

Our neighbours, Tessa and Derek, considered themselves to be connoisseurs (?) of supermarket wines.

See if we can convey the same incredulity in a rewrite:

Despite widespread views to the contrary, our neighbours Tessa and Derek considered themselves to be connoisseurs of supermarket wines.

Too wordy? Then try this simple expedient:

Our neighbours Tessa and Derek considered themselves to be 'connoisseurs' of supermarket wines.

A problem for many people is whether words that follow a question mark should be capitalised or not. Their confusion may arise by occasionally seeing what is sometimes called the 'internal question mark':

Why should she get the reward? the Daily Mail asks today.

*What will happen to the whale's carcass? is the question on
the lips of most beachside residents.*

This usage is probably a carryover from common practice
a couple of centuries ago. Here, for example, is a sentence from
Dr Johnson's preface to his *Dictionary* (1785):

*But what makes a word obsolete, more than general
agreement to forbear it? and how shall it be continued . . .*

Or, again, in Jane Austen's *Pride and Prejudice* (1813):

*" What say you, Mary? for you are a lady of deep reflection,
I know, and read great books . . . "*

The Fowlers, in *The King's English*, are right to call this usage
ugly in modern prose and suggest that a question mark should
always be followed by a capital. Taking our earlier examples, it
isn't too difficult to rewrite them as straightforward indirect
questions requiring no question marks:

*Today the Daily Mail asks whether or not she should get the
reward.*

*What happens to the whale's carcass is the question on the
lips of most beachside residents.*

The Exclamation Mark!

Exiled in Guernsey during the 1860s and desperate to find out how his new novel *Les Misérables* was selling, the French writer Victor Hugo sent a telegram to his publisher bearing a single symbol: '?'. His equally frugal publisher replied in kind:'!' .

Today the exclamation mark is hardly known for witty usage. It is discouraged, if not banned, by modern newspapers (where it is referred to as a 'startler', 'gasper', 'screamer', and by tabloid sub-editors as a 'dog's dick'), and with a reputation for over-use, the mark nevertheless earns its keep with a surprisingly wide range of legitimate uses.

It's difficult to imagine the following examples conveying anything like the same force and feeling without the screamers:

Shut up!   You bitch!   What a mess!   Damn!

And literature would undoubtedly be the poorer without them. Good writers aren't afraid of exclamation marks and use them judiciously for a number of functions:

CONVEYING ANGER,   *You're out of your mind!*
SCORN AND DISGUST   *You must be joking!*
   How dare you even breathe her name!

INDICATING IRONY AND REVERSE MEANING	*Thanks a lot!* *That's bloody lovely, that is!*
UNDERLINING INSULTS AND EXPLETIVES	*You bastard!* *Shit!*
CONVEYING IRONIC TONE	*You're not so smart!* *And you said we wouldn't win!* *Don't do anything I wouldn't do!*
COMMANDING	*Come here! Right now!* *Get lost! And don't ever come back!*

With all these examples, the statements would be bland and colourless without the exclamation marks. And some would be completely meaningless:

Don't do anything I wouldn't do.

Substitute an exclamation mark for the full stop and the statement acquires the intended 'raised eyebrow' or 'nudge, nudge' tone to become the idiomatic invitation to have a really good time. Misuse of the exclamation mark undoubtedly contributes to its overuse. None of the following examples requires it:

When she heard the result, Shirley almost fainted!
Peter managed to get a job at the bakery!
When they finally arrived, the plants were all damaged!

Alas, such examples are all too common. It's worth remembering H W Fowler's warning: 'Excessive use of exclamation marks in expository prose is a certain indication of an unpractised writer or of one who wants to add a spurious dash of sensation to something unsensational'. Always think twice before using an exclamation mark, and think twenty times before using it in multiples:

> *Patricia went to Venice – again! That's the second time in a year!! And you'll never guess who she met there!!!*

Avoiding Catastrophes
with Apostrophes

Who hasn't chortled over everyday apostrophic clangers
such as these:

Cig's, Crisp's, Snack's etc	– Roadside cafe sign
Lilie's, Anemone's and Mum's	– East London florist
Fresh asparagu's	– Edinburgh greengrocer
Bargain Mens Shirt's	– Market sign
Ocean Fresh Crab Stix's	– Fishmonger's sign
Her's is a warm, informal home.	– Newspaper interview
This school and it's playground will be closed over Easter	– Sign on Croydon school gate

Of course it's easy to take the high grammatical ground but
if we're honest most of us have to admit that there are times when
we're forced to think quite hard about the use – and misuse – of
apostrophes. So what's the problem? The problem lies simply in
the ability to recognise that there are two – and only two – kinds
of apostrophes. One kind indicates the possession of something;

the other kind indicates a contraction or abbreviation – a letter or letters left out of a word:

POSSESSIVE APOSTROPHE   *Did you know **Jack's car** is a write-off?*

*I heard that **Jack's kids** have the flu.*

CONTRACTION APOSTROPHE   *Did you know that **Jack's** had an accident?*

*I heard that **Jack's** in hospital.*

*I heard that **Jack'll** be out tomorrow.*

In the first two examples the apostrophes tell us that the car and the kids belong to Jack; they are **possessive apostrophes**. In the last three examples the apostrophes signal to us that something has been left out; that *Jack's* and *Jack'll* are shortened versions of two or more words:

***Jack's** had an accident*	=	***Jack has** had an accident.*
***Jack's** in hospital*	=	***Jack is** in hospital.*
***Jack'll** be out tomorrow*	=	***Jack will** be out tomorrow.*

These last examples *(Jack's, Jack'll)* are called **contraction apostrophes**. We're *(We are)* expected to work out what these mean, and with a little experience we soon learn to identify them and to fill in the gaps:

My God! Did you hear? London's burning!
*(**Contraction:** London **is** burning).*

*I hope London's fire services can cope! (***Possessive:*** the fire services that belong to or are situated in London).*

*She'd be here if she could (***Contraction:*** She **would** be here if she could).*

*It's nobody's fault, really. (***Contraction:*** It is; ***Possessive:*** the fault of nobody).*

In the mid-1990s there was a threat by British Airways to buy part of the Australian airline Qantas. Antipodean feelings ran high and a protest group erected a huge sign on the perimeter of Sydney's international airport:

PUBLIC NOTICE
NO BRITISH AIRWAYS OWNERSHIP OF
OUR QANTAS
PISS OFF POM'S

The highly (and internationally) visible admonition drew a torrent of complaints about the language on the big sign; not, however, objecting to the crude language suggesting that the British should forthwith depart, but rather about the redundant apostrophe in 'Poms'!

Possessive Apostrophes

You may understand possessive apostrophes a little better if you know how they came about. Before 1500, possession was indicated by a phrase which went something like, 'the Bishop, his cassock'. In time, this was shortened to 'the Bishopis cassock' and then to the way it was pronounced, 'the Bishops cassock' but written 'the Bishop's cassock' with a raised comma to show that a letter had been dropped. And that is how the possessive (or genitive) apostrophe has come down to us today:

> *Joyce's house, Bill's lawnmower, a boy's bike, Michael's*
> *holiday, his uncle's car, her grandfather's clock*

Possession, ownership or association can apply not only to people but also to things and abstractions:

> *a good day's work, the company's policy, the tree's branches,*
> *a door's hinges, an idea's validity, a moment's notice*

And the same goes for certain plural nouns:

> *men's trousers, children's toys, mice's*
> *tails, the people's favourite*

No problems there. But you'll notice that all the above examples have something in common: none of the possessor words or names ends with an 's' – *Joyce, boy, Michael, uncle, grandfather, day, company, men, mice, people,* etc. So what's the problem about words ending with an 's'?

The problem is that adding possessive apostrophes to words and names such as *boss, surplus, Thomas,* and to plurals such as *cats, hours and friends,* is not such a straightforward business. Let's look at some examples:

SINGULAR WORDS AND NAMES ENDING WITH 'S'	POSSESSIVE FORM
the boss	*the boss's temper*
Thomas	*Thomas's recent illness*
mistress	*a mistress's secrets*
Charles Dickens	*Dickens's novels*

So far, so good. But now see what happens when *plural nouns* that end with 's' become possessive:

PLURAL WORDS AND NAMES ENDING WITH 'S'	POSSESSIVE FORM
her **friends**	her **friends'** parties
Penny's **parents**	Penny's **parents'** cottage
the **members**	the **members'** privileges
our **employees**	our **employees'** bonuses
the **girls**	the **girls'** classroom

Get the picture? For singular possession we simply add 's, but for plural or shared possession we add the apostrophe *after* the s – **s'**. This system enables us to distinguish different intended meanings. When we read,

*The visiting opera star heard the **girl's** singing.*

we are being told that the star listened to only one girl singing, whereas

*The visiting opera star heard the **girls'** singing.*

tells us (if we've learned the rules!) that the diva listened to many girls singing.

Remember, however, that those plurals we discussed earlier – those not ending with 's' – require the apostrophe to be placed before the 's' and not after: *the women's changing room; the old folk's belongings*.

In some cases, especially with names, we have choices, according to taste. We can add the final **'s** *(Tom Jones's songs, Prince Charles's opinions)* or drop it *(Wales' ruggedness, Dickens' characters, Jesus' teachings)*. And there are many cases which, for one reason or another, observe rigid tradition. For example it is *Queens' College, Cambridge*, but *Queen's College, Oxford*. Here are a few more oddities:

WITH A POSSESSIVE APOSTROPHE	*Lord's Cricket Ground, St John's Wood, St John's (Newfoundland), St Michael's Mount, Regent's Park, St Katharine's Dock, Court of St James's, King's Cross, Land's End, St Giles' Cathedral, Christie's and Sotheby's, King's College, London.*
WITHOUT A POSSESSIVE APOSTROPHE	*Earls Court, St Kitts, Golders Green, Shepherds Bush, St Andrews University, St Helens (Lancashire), Missing Persons Bureau, Pears soap, Gas Consumers Council.*

We can assume that all these examples began life as proper possessives. Many have retained their apostrophe even though the possession has gone missing; we say (and spell) *Cruft's* (dog show); *Lord's* (cricket ground); *Christie's* (auction house).

But somewhat more perplexing is that while *Lloyd's of London* and *Lloyd's Register of Shipping* retain their apostrophes (and are referred to as *Lloyd's*), *Lloyds Bank* decided years ago to chuck theirs away and is referred to as *Lloyds*!

Pronouns and Possessive Apostrophes

So far we've dealt with the problems of possessive nouns and proper nouns. But pronouns can be troublesome, too: some have apostrophes and some do not:

PRONOUNS WITH APOSTROPHES	*one's problems, anyone's idea, someone's shoes, one another's responsibilities, nobody's fault, anybody's luggage, each other's possessions*
PRONOUNS WITHOUT APOSTROPHES	*his, hers, its, ours, yours, theirs*

One of the most frequent errors is the use of *it's* for the possessive form of *it*. This is wrong, of course: *it's* is the accepted contraction for *it is* or *it has*.

Apostrophic Enigmas

If, after absorbing all the rules about apostophising you still experience problems about where to place that raised comma, you are not alone. A year never passes without a – often lengthy – war of words breaking out in the national broadsheets concerning the finer and disputable points of apostrophe usage. Here is one to ponder:

> *Steve Davis, the snooker player and friend of the boxer's, said:*
> *"Frank used to be regarded as the Eddie the Eagle of boxing;*
> *now he's Roy of the Rovers."*   *– The Times , 4/9/95*

. . . *a friend of the boxer's?* A friend of the boxer's what?
The boxer in question here is Frank Bruno, but the real question
is what possession does the possessive apostrophe refer to?
Yet the usage is correct: it is just another way of saying *Steve Davis,
the snooker player and the boxer's friend* . . . In other words the
'missing' possession referred to by the apostrophe is 'the friendship
of Steve Davis'.

Here's another example of what is called by some the
double possessive, in a letter to *The Times*:

> *My sympathy is with the train drivers in their present
> dispute. Last week you compared their wages with bus
> driver's. I fail to see the similarity.*

Here the object of the possessive apostrophe is easier to
track: *the bus driver's* **wages**. A final example, from *The Sunday Times*
(22/5/94):

> *If I had the slightest interest in making my biography of
> Kenneth Branagh and Emma Thompson a work of
> speculative salaciousness, I could do worse than model my
> approach on Stuart Wavell's.*

It's fairly clear that by referring to the preceding text that it
is Wavell's biographical approach that is being deprecated here.
Those examples may help you with possessive nouns and names
where the possession appears to have gone missing; but it isn't all

plain sailing; there are grammar radicals out there who don't buy the inserted apostrophe at all. Only recently English Heritage was roundly criticised for having written in its castle guidebooks that 'this was the home of the Neville's or the Scott's or the whoever's'. This objection appears to be made in the mistaken belief that the apostrophes are redundantly inserted into the plural names (as in the infamous *potatoe's* and *tomatoe's*) but surely the apostrophes here are legitimately *possessive* – indicating the *Neville family's home*, the *Scott family's home*, etc.

 If you have to deal with a plural possessive, you couldn't do better than study this fine example of grammatical elegance in a letter to *The Times*:

> *Sir, Today at Balsham I buried William Jolly, aged 107, born 1886, in which year at Balsham was buried Mary Brown, aged 93, born 1793 – two lives' spans that take us back into the 18th century.*
> *Yours faithfully, Rev W N C Girard, The Rectory, Balsham, Cambridgeshire, 10/11/93.*

Now, what about pronouns? Spot the error in this parliamentary report:

> *On Friday she (Lady Olga Maitland) had said the amendments were her's and on Monday said that although she had sought consultation it would be unfair to suggest that they came from other sources.*

Refer back to the list of pronouns without apostrophes (*his, hers, its, ours, yours and theirs*) and you'll see that it should be *the amendments were **hers** and not *her's*.

We noted earlier that *Lloyd's* (not *Lloyds Bank*) carries a possessive apostrophe – standing for *Lloyd's* coffee house, the place where the famous London insurance house began business in the 17th century. In this context you may care to ponder this unusual example of apostrophe usage, from an article in *The Times*:

> *Sally Knowles, a name, said: "When is Lloyd's going to accept that their's has been a society of overpaid incompetents and cunning, greedy people who make double-glazing and time-share salesmen look like amateurs?"*

These are unusually strong words but the most unusual word is *their's*. We have noted that *theirs* is a pronoun that never carries a possessive apostrophe, so how can this usage presume to be correct? There is an argument that as *Lloyd's* stands for *Lloyds [Society of Underwriters]*, a 'double possessive' pronoun is required: *their's*.

This is wrong, as would be *a friend of my father's*, where the *'s* is redundant (*a friend of my father* says it correctly), although a seemingly similar expression – *that story of Fred's* (ie *Fred's story*) is of course legitimate.

On the subject of enigmatic apostrophes, how do you handle group possessives? Is it *my aunt's and uncle's family*, or *my aunt and uncle's family*? Here's an example:

> *As academics, Dr Gill and Dr Chippendale's first aim is to inform other archaelogists, government officials and museum curators.*

This usage is acceptable and the meaning is quite clear. Dr Gill and Dr Chippendale (or less usually, *Drs Gill and Chippendale*) share a common aim. But watch this usage carefully. *Louise and Spencer's parents* is understood to mean that Louise and Spencer share the same parents, while *Louise's and Spencer's parents* means they have different parents.

Finally, here are a few posers quoted in H W Fowler's *Modern English Usage*. The examples are cited as solutions to apostrophe problems, not rulings carved in stone:

> *Wayne's daughter Kim's latex ear.*
>
> *Its [Burger King's] decision was not unexpected.*
>
> *Michael's mother's new boyfriend.*
>
> *A former boxer ignores Gillespie (Carroll O'Connor)'s advice.*
>
> *It's Ronnie Finney, Fatty Finney's brother's son's second boy. [Phew!]*

Contraction Apostrophes

George Bernard Shaw, campaigning for simplified spelling and punctuation, tried to encourage the nation to do without contraction apostrophes – *cant, wont, arent,* etc – but where he failed, the *Washington Post* succeeded spectacularly, though unwittingly. According to the American author Bill Bryson, the newspaper once published an article which confused the possessive *its* with the contraction *it's* no less than five times in a couple of paragraphs:

> *Its the worst its been in the last five years . . . Its awful . . . Its come full circle . . . Its nice to see the enemy . . .*

One of the most frequent errors is the use of *it's* for the possessive form of *it*. This is wrong, of course: *it's* is the accepted contraction for *it is* or *it has*. For the record:

POSSESSION   *The newspaper claimed **its** punctuation record was unmatched by any of **its** rivals.*

CONTRACTION   ***It's** (It is) a fact that the punctuation record of the newspaper **isn't** (is not) so clever after all.*

Also for the record is this list of most of the accepted contractions, many of which have been in use for centuries – *don't* (1670), *can't* (1706), *ain't* (1778), *shan't* (1850), *I've* (1885):

aren't	*are not*	*she'll*	*she will, she shall*
can't	*cannot, can not*	*she's*	*she is, she has*
couldn't	*could not*	*there's*	*there is*
hasn't	*has not*	*they'll*	*they will, they shall*
haven't	*have not*	*they're*	*they are*
he'll	*he will, he shall*	*they've*	*they have*
he's	*he is, he has*	*we'll*	*we will, we shall*
I'd	*I would, I had*	*weren't*	*were not*
I'm	*I am*	*who's*	*who is, who has*
it's	*it is, it has*	*won't*	*will not*
I've	*I have*	*wouldn't*	*would not*
let's	*let us*	*you'll*	*you will, you shall*
ma'am	*madam*	*you're*	*you are*
mustn't	*must not*	*you've*	*you have*

As you can see, *who's* is short for *who is* or *who has* – but *whose* indicates possession: *Whose wallet is this?*

There are many more idiomatic contractions: *sweet'n'low,* *'alf a mo', finger lickin', rock'n'roll,* and so forth. Some antique contractions barely survive: *o'er* (over), *ne'er* (never), and *e'en* (even). But quite a few common words formerly carrying contraction apostrophes (*'cello, 'flu, 'phone,* for *violoncello, influenza* and *telephone*) are now accepted without them.

Out, damned squiggle! out, I say!

Yes, apostrophes of either kind are tricky little squiggles, so don't be too disheartened if you are occasionally stumped by them. If it's any consolation, even the experts are frequently humiliated by apostrophic clangers. Here are some from a 1996 school inspector's report, for which the Office for Standards in Education was forced to apologise:

> *. . . pupils work is carefully and regularly marked . . .*
> (missing)
>
> *. . . some insights into children's' progress . . .* (two for good measure)
>
> *. . . errors occur within individual's work . . .* (misplaced)

And here are some more, from a Cheshire Library Association publication:

> *One third of all 14 year old's have a reading age of 11 or less, while 40% of 16-19 year old's in further education lack basic literacy and numeracy skills.*

The pot calling the kettle black? Little wonder there are frequent calls for the resurrection of the Society for the Preservation of Apostrophes (SPA) although in the light of the above example perhaps there should be another – the Society for the Extermination of Redundant Apostrophes (SERA).

Spot the Apostrophe Catastrophes!

1. My car's a Ford. Whats your's?

2. Ethel claimed that the jacket was her's.

3. Pay nothing til' after Easter.

4. Seasons Greetings from Sainsbury's.

5. It's the countries largest supermarket.

6. Thomas's love affair with Jeans sister is off.

7. Railtrack welcome's you to Leeds City Station.

8. Pupils expectations today are too low.

9. Georg Solti was one of the centurys greatest maestro's.

10. The campaign collapsed during it's final stages.

Answers.   1. An apostrophe required in *what's* (what is) but not in *yours*. 2. No apostrophe in *hers*. 3. The apostrophe should be moved in front of *'til* to indicate the abbreviation of *until*. 4. A possessive apostrophe is required in *Season's*. 5. Should be *country's*. 6. Possessive apostrophe required for *Jean's*. 7. No apostrophe in *welcomes*. 8. The plural *Pupils'* requires a possessive apostrophe. 9. Possessive apostrophe needed for *century's* but not in the plural *maestros*. 10. *Its* is a possessive pronoun which has no apostrophe.

Quotation Marks

Although **quotation marks** are often called 'inverted commas', if you look closely you will see that they are not. You'll see that only the opening mark is inverted – that is, with the tail of the squiggle pointing up; the closing mark is a normal raised or hanging comma, or pair of commas. So we should use the term *quotation marks* (or *quotes* for short) exclusively.

Another thing you'll note in your general reading is that there are two kinds of quotation marks – single ('single') and double ("double"):

> *Heather declared flatly, 'I never want to see Jim again.'*
> *Heather declared flatly, "I never want to see Jim again."*

Is there a reason for using one or the other? It's a very confusing issue, and newspaper and book publishers are divided on it. Some, like virtually all US publishers and in this country *The Times*, *The Sun* and the *Independent*, prefer double quotes, while *The Mail* and the *Observer* opt for single quotes. Book publishers are just as split on the choice. Defenders of the single mark point to the advantages of simplified and attractive typography, but double mark enthusiasts insist they have logic on their side. If, for example, they say, you read the following:

One of the commissioners gave it as his opinion that the value of the euro in 1999 would be 'over the top'.

would you know for sure whether the commissioner was being quoted and actually said 'over the top'? Or would you take it that his comments were being summarised by the phrase 'over the top'? We simply don't know. Proponents of the double quotation mark to indicate direct speech, leaving the single quotation marks for all other purposes, do have a point.

But whether you use double or single marks you need to be aware of the convention for enclosing a quoted passage within another. If you use single marks, an additional direct speech quotation within your first quotation must be enclosed within double marks (or vice versa if you are a double-mark user):

The sales assistant said, 'We only have them in grey and blue but yesterday my boss told me, "I don't know why they don't make them in other colours".'

On the rare occasions where it is found necessary to have a third quote within a second quote in the same sentence, the formula is double/single/double, or single/double/single.

Quoting Direct Speech

Although the authorised version of the Bible is abuzz with speeches, dialogue and discussion, there is not a single quotation mark in sight.

This would hardly do today. When we read a newspaper report or an interview or even fiction we want to know when we're reading reported or paraphrased speech, and when we're reading words *actually spoken*. The most important role of quotation marks is to help us differentiate between the two forms:

> *Mr Murphy said that in his view the value of the pound would drop towards the end of the year. "I also believe most European currencies will follow suit," he added.*

This clearly tells us that the writer has summarised the first part of Mr Murphy's statement in his own words, and we have to accept that his summary is an accurate interpretation of what Mr Murphy said. But we should have no doubts about the accuracy of the second part of the statement because the quotation marks tell us that the words printed between them are actually those spoken by Mr Murphy.

When you are quoting direct speech you must ensure that the words enclosed by your quotation marks are *exactly* those spoken. Not approximately, but *exactly*. Important – and costly – legal actions have been won and lost on this point.

This is fairly fundamental, yet it is surprising how many people, including some famous writers, get it wrong. The English language expert J E Metcalf, who delighted in exposing the solecisms of the famous, loved to quote errant passages from Jane Austen's classic novel, *Persuasion*:

> *Anne mentioned the glimpses she had had of him at Lyme, but without being much attended to. "Oh, yes, perhaps, it had been Mr Elliot. They did not know. It might be him, perhaps."*

144

> *Sir Walter thought much of Mrs Wallis; she was said to be*
> *an excessively pretty woman; beautiful. "He longed to see her.*
> *He hoped she might make some amends for the many plain*
> *faces he was continually passing in the streets. The worst of*
> *Bath was, the number of its plain women . . . "*

It's obvious that the first quotation is not of direct speech and could not have actually been spoken by Anne. If Anne was being quoted it would read differently: *"Oh yes, perhaps, it could have been Mr Elliot. I don't know. It could have been him, perhaps."* The second quotation purports to be words spoken by Anne about Sir Walter but, again, the form of expression is hardly that of directly quoted speech; it is rather a summation. Jane Austen's decidedly aberrant use of quotation marks in *Persuasion* is among English literature's more intriguing mysteries.

You can see endless possibilities for confusion, can't you? Look at these two almost similar sentences:

- *Jones stated that 'he was innocent of the crime.'*
- *Jones stated that he was 'innocent of the crime'.*

In the first example, Jones did not say 'I was innocent' but that 'he was innocent'. By this we are free to assume that Jones, by referring to 'he', is talking about another person whom he says is innocent of a crime. It could also mean that the writer or reporter hasn't used the quotation marks correctly – we'll never know. But in the second example the words uttered by Jones – those enclosed in quotation marks – unequivocally tell us that Jones, in his own words, has claimed that he is innocent of the crime. Of course it could all be made completely clear by a quotation of direct speech:

● *Jones stated, 'I am innocent of the crime.'*

Such examples stress the importance of making sure that your reader knows who is responsible for the quoted statement. This is usually accomplished by what is called a *reporting clause*, which can introduce the statement or follow it or even interrupt it:

● **Jones stated,** *"I am innocent and I can easily prove it."*

● *"I am innocent and I can easily prove it,"* **Jones stated**.

● *"I am innocent,"* **Jones stated**, *"and I can easily prove it."*

A couple of other points worth noting:

● Even if the quoted speech is limited to a single word, the same rules apply: *The doctor described the patient's recovery as "extraordinary".*

● With long quotations that extend beyond a paragraph, use only an opening quotation mark at the start of each new paragraph. Use the closing quotation mark only at the very end of the quoted statement, even if it's half a dozen paragraphs away.

● It is usual to introduce quotations with a comma or a colon: *Theodora sighed, 'I've felt so tired lately.'* ... *Theodora sighed: 'I've felt so tired lately.'*

And a final important point. When quoted speech is interrupted by a reporting clause, two rules apply. If the quoted statement is interrupted at the end of a sentence it should be finished with a comma and resumed with a capital letter:

> *"I knew I'd seen that bird before," said Gavin. "It was a cormorant, wasn't it?"*

But if the speech is interrupted mid-sentence, it should be resumed in lower-case:

> *"Don't you agree," asked Gavin, "that the bird over there is a cormorant?"*

How to Close Quotations

Most writers soon learn that once you begin a quotation of direct speech using opening quotation marks, you must also close it. As with enclosing parentheses or brackets, the marks, whether single or double, always operate in pairs.

What is a little more difficult is . . . *how*? Look at this example:

> *Louis then asked her, "Do you think I'm drunk"?*

Do you place the question mark *outside* the quotation mark that closes the direct speech, or *inside*?

Louis then asked her, "Do you think I'm drunk?"

The answer is that it depends on the relationship between the quotation and the sentence that contains it. The rule is worth engraving on the memory:

> PUNCTUATION MARKS (full stops, commas, question and exclamation marks, etc) GO **INSIDE** THE FINAL QUOTATION MARK IF THEY RELATE TO THE QUOTED WORDS, BUT **OUTSIDE** IF THEY RELATE TO THE WHOLE SENTENCE.

In our example, the question mark relates only to the quoted statement, *"Do you think I'm drunk?"* and so it rightly belongs *inside* the final quotation mark, *not* outside. But let's change the sentence slightly:

Should Louis have asked her, "Do you think I'm drunk"?

Here, if you remember the rule, you can see that the question is an essential part of the whole sentence, and so the question mark *outside* the final quotation mark is correct. To be pedantic, the sentence should properly be written like this:

Should Louis have asked her, "Do you think I'm drunk?"?

Here you see that the quotation has its own question mark *inside* the final quotation mark (quite correctly), and the overall sentence has its mark *outside* (again correctly).

148

But the two piggybacked question marks look a bit silly and everyone accepts that in a case like this the inside question mark can be dropped without causing confusion.

It must be said that the rules governing the placing of quotation marks and punctuation are a bit arbitrary. For this reason it might be worth noting what is regarded as acceptable:

● **Single words.** A single word quoted within a sentence isn't normally entitled to its own closing stop, whether a full stop or other mark; they belong to the whole sentence:

WRONG   *Melvyn remarked that Veronica was a "gossip."*

CORRECT   *Melvyn remarked that Veronica was a "gossip".*

● **Phrases and incomplete sentences.** Any quotation short of a complete sentence would not normally have its own stop – unless the sense dictated otherwise:

WRONG   *Bill was always promising Alice that he'd give her "the shirt off his back!"*

CORRECT   *Bill was always promising Alice that he'd give her "the shirt off his back"!*

● **Quote ends at the same point as the enclosing sentence.** This bothers a lot of writers because if the quotation is a complete sentence then logically two separate stops are required: one relating to the quoted sentence and the other to the sentence as a whole. There's nothing grammatically wrong in using both stops but it is accepted that we drop one of them – usually the stop *outside* the final quotation mark.

FUSSY	*Louis tried to tell her, "I think I'm drunk.".*
BETTER	*Louis tried to tell her, "I think I'm drunk."*

● **Quote is interrupted within the sentence.**

If a quotation is interrupted at a point where it has its own punctuation, a comma is normally substituted for the punctuation. Let's say the words to be quoted are *Live all you can; it's a mistake not to*. Here's how it would be treated if broken off and resumed:

WRONG	*"Live all you can;" advised Henry James, "it's a mistake not to."*
CORRECT	*"Live all you can," advised Henry James, "it's a mistake not to."*

You'll note that the comma following *can* is *outside* the quotation mark; that is because it is not part of the original quotation. However there is an alternative treatment. The reporting clause *(advised Henry James)* could be followed by a semicolon, although hardly by a full stop – that would require *it's* to begin with a capital letter which would be unfaithful to the original quotation.

● **Quotation consists of more than one sentence.**

If the quoted material consists of two or more sentences, then they retain their original punctuation. Note that the final punctuation mark (a full stop in this case) is *within* the final quotation mark:

CORRECT	*It was the poet Wallace Stevens who observed that "Frogs Eat Butterflies. Snakes Eat Frogs. Hogs Eat Snakes. Men Eat Hogs."*

● **Other matter relating to a quotation.** Generally, any mark or matter that is part of the quotation stays *within* the quotation marks. Even if certain matter relates closely to the quotation, if it isn't part of the quote then place it *outside* the quotation marks:

WRONG   *Matt went on and on about the match. "If only that referee had half a brain"* . . . *The others agreed.*

CORRECT   *Matt went on and on about the match. "If only that referee had half a brain* . . . *" The others agreed.*

CORRECT   *Claud Cockburn claimed he wrote the world's dullest newspaper headline: "Small earthquake in Chile. Not many dead." (In Time of Trouble, 1956.)*

British and American Punctuation

With an increasing number of American-published and printed books circulating in Britain it is understandable that some of the aforegoing rules could cause confusion. They are, in fact, quotation practices peculiar to British English. American English (and that of some Commonwealth countries) adopts a significantly different rule about quotation marks.

Generally, quotation marks in British English aim to be logical in that they are placed according to sense and context. Their placement in American English may lack logic but does have the virtue of simplicity: *all punctuation* (stops, commas, colons and semicolons, exclamation and question marks, etc) *precedes all final quotation marks*.

Compare the following examples:

ENGLISH QUOTATION MARKS	AMERICAN QUOTATION MARKS
Dr Johnson described a lexicographer as "a harmless drudge".	*Dr Johnson described a lexicographer as "a harmless drudge."*
Dr Johnson said that a lexicographer was "a harmless drudge", yet was himself one.	*Dr Johnson said that a lexicographer was "a harmless drudge," yet was himself one.*
The lecturer said that "Dr Johnson described a lexicographer as 'a harmless drudge'."	*The lecturer said that "Dr Johnson described a lexicographer as 'a harmless drudge.' "*

With the increasing globalisation of publishing, many British publishers are switching to the American model.

Direct Speech: Style and Ethics

In many circumstances, the practice of relating what people say has the power to infuse veracity, life and immediacy into your prose. This is something you might hesitate to do in personal or business letters, but which would be appropriate, and even refreshing, in many kinds of fiction and non-fiction writing.

Take this descriptive passage, for example:

I was surprised to hear that my wife's Uncle Ted and Auntie Gwen were getting divorced. They are both in their late 80s and only last year celebrated their 60th wedding anniversary.

Apparently one of their problems was to convince the divorce court that they really did wish to get divorced and, if so, on what grounds, after all this time together. I heard that when asked this, Auntie Gwen told the judge that she'd had quite enough of married life with Uncle Ted.

It's an interesting story, but the way it's told leaves the reader a bit flat. Uncle Ted and especially Auntie Gwen must be, in these unusual circumstances, a couple of real characters, but this isn't conveyed at all. And the ending is lame, leaving the reader with a sense of being cheated of a good punchline.

Without changing the facts of the account, why not replay the court scene in your head, imagining the characters involved and *hearing* what they are saying – or might be saying. Put this down on paper and see what a difference it makes.

I was surprised to hear that my wife's Uncle Ted and Auntie Gwen were getting divorced. But apparently they faced some problems trying to convince the divorce court that they really did wish to split up for good. The judge could hardly believe it.

"How old are you?" she asked Auntie Gwen.

"I'm eighty-six," she told the judge, who then asked Uncle Ted to state his age.

"Eighty-eight," said Uncle Ted.

"And how long have you been married?"

"Sixty-two years," Auntie Gwen told her.

"Sixty-two years!" said the judge in disbelief. "And after all this time you want to get divorced?"

I'm told that Auntie Gwen turned to the judge, shook her head, and said, "Look, Judge, enough is enough."

153

Finally, on using quotations, here's the advice that *The Times* gives its journalists:

> *The sloppy use of quotes is the bane of good writing. A well-chosen quote can electrify a passage. Equally it can distort what a speaker said. As a rule, a quote must be attributed to a person, with full name and the date and place of quotation. Unattributed quotes are normally banned. Where they proliferate, for instance in the more pedestrian political reporting, they should be treated with caution. Many readers are inclined to believe they are made up. An unattributed quote should be used only where confidentiality is clearly essential, not merely to add spice and colour to a story.*

Other Functions of Quotation Marks

Most punctuation marks are multi-functional and quotation marks are no exception. Here are some other ways in which they are used:

TO INDICATE TITLES
She said she'd seen the recipe in Delia Smith's 'Summer Collection' Alan's favourite film was the Marx Brothers' classic, 'Duck Soup'.

TO IDENTIFY NICKNAMES
Henry 'Rabbit Punch' Watson. Beulah 'Bubbles' Henley-Howard. Al 'Scarface' Capone.

TO INDICATE DOUBT, CYNICISM, DISBELIEF, IRONY
The hamburgers contained a blend of liver, chicken parts and 'organic beef'. The spokesman inferred that lawyers were, on the whole, charitable; but most people would hesitate before throwing themselves on the mercy of 'charitable' lawyers.

TO INDICATE THAT A WORD OR PHRASE SHOULD NOT BE TAKEN LITERALLY

We are 'giving away' this nationally advertised Pyramid X100 Fresh Air Ioniser for only £19.99!

Punctuation Pot-pourri: ellipsis, asterisks, bullets, strokes and typographical effects

We're now sifting through the detritus of punctuation but there are still nuggets to be found: a few dots here, a stroke there, stars, bullets and daggers . . . all of which can be put to work on occasional odd jobs.

The Three-dot Ellipsis

The science fiction pioneer H G Wells has been credited with the invention of this mark . . . but wait! What about that deathless cry from the dramatised version of Mrs Henry Wood's *East Lynne:* 'Dead! and . . . never called me mother', published in 1874 and antedating H G Wells's claim by at least a couple of decades. But let's not quibble over a mark so ridiculously simple that it's hard to believe it needed inventing at all: the **three-dot ellipsis**. What this line of dots does is indicate missing matter, which may consist of a single word:

> *Get the . . . out of here!*

or matter considered to be non-essential:

> *Yesterday the shares stood at just over £4.65 which if you believe last night's closing statement . . . at that price the company is valued at almost £1.6 billion.*

or an implied quotation or phrase which the reader is expected to know:

> *So then she bought contact lenses: you know, men don't make passes . . . And she actually believes that, too!*

or indicating an unfinished thought:

> *The troubling question was, would Mrs Benedict sue, or . . .*

or indicating a time lapse:

> *Kimball crashed to the floor with eye-wincing force . . . only later, much later, in the darkness, did the realisation come to him that he was now a marked man.*

or indicating disjointed speech:

> *She paced the room. 'I don't know . . . every way I look at it . . . what would you do, Charles?' She drew deeply on her cigarette. 'I mean, surely he wouldn't do this to me . . . or would he?'*

The Asterisk

This complaining letter to *The Times* should adequately explain one of the most useful functions of the **asterisk**:

> *In your paper last week I noticed a f***, a b***** and a f***ing and this made me wonder just who you think comprises your readership. If you feel that you have to censor any word that could possibly upset anybody, why do we not have M****** H****tine, the M********t Treaty and the C****n Ag*********l P****y?**

The final asterisk is in its customary role of guiding the reader to a footnote or explanation elsewhere in the text, thus:

* *Michael Heseltine, Maastricht Treaty, Common Agricultural Policy.*

Bullets

In our busy age the **bullet** point (●) has found increasing favour, perhaps because:

- It enables us to summarise clearly a series of facts or conclusions.

- It sends a signal to the eye that 'here are the essentials'.

- It encourages writers to be brief, and to use single words and phrases rather than long sentences.

- It captures readers who are too lazy or too harassed to read solid texts.

The Stroke

Fancily called the virgule, solidus, shilling mark, slash, diagonal and separatrix, the oblique **stroke** has a few limited uses:

TO INDICATE OPTIONS *It depends upon how he/she behaves.*
The situation calls for guile and/or force.

TO SEPARATE LINES OF VERSE *The mist as it rises / touched with gold of the morning / Veils over the sadness / and the spirit lifts, soaring . . .*

TO ABBREVIATE *A/c = account; C/o = care of; km/hr = kilometres per hour.*

Italics, Bold and Underlining

As tools for separating, highlighting and clarifying text, these devices are on the margins of punctuation. Although they can hardly apply to handwritten text, in this word-processing age the *italic*, **bold** and underline keys make possible a range of useful typographic effects. Most of them have been used in this book:

FOR EMPHASIS Do **not** use a capital letter after a colon. *Its* is a possessive pronoun and *never* has an apostrophe.

TO DISTINGUISH A WORD OR WORD GROUP Less than a century ago, tomorrow was hyphenated as to-morrow.

159

TO IDENTIFY EXTRACTS AND QUOTATIONS

The Collins English Dictionary describes an adjective as **a word imputing a characteristic to a noun or pronoun**.

TO INDICATE TITLES

Several errors involving quotation marks will be found in Jane Austen's *Persuasion*.

TO INDICATE A FOREIGN WORD OR PHRASE

The movement's meetings were always heavy with *Sturm und Drang*, shouting and arguing.

It's worth noting that once a foreign word or phrase is generally understood and accepted into the English language (remember that English is and always has been a shameless global word burglar) it need not be italicised or highlighted. Such words include, for example, *guru*, *vis-à-vis*, *sauerkraut*, *patisserie*, *shiatsu* and *flamenco*. If in doubt a good dictionary will guide you.

The Numbers Game: Punctuating Numbers and Figures

Writing and communicating isn't confined to letters and words. Numbers figure largely in our lives, too: money, time, dates, measurements, locations. And as with any spoken or written communication it is essential that numerical expressions are clearly understood.So the principle behind the punctuation of numbers is simply this: seek clarity; eliminate ambiguity.

When to spell out numbers.

Numbers from one to ten are generally spelled out; thereafter *11, 23, 785* etc. Round numbers and approximate amounts can be expressed in words or figures, according to taste:

- *Nearly six hundred feet high; she was in her early eighties; the population was well over two million; three or four feet long.*

- *Nearly 600 ft high; she was in her early 80s; the population was well over 2,000,000 (or 2m); 3-4 ft long.*

Avoid beginning sentences with numerals; they look better spelled out:

UGLY   *160 deer were culled on the estate last week.*

BETTER   *A hundred and sixty deer were culled on the estate last week.*

Alternatively, rewrite the sentence to avoid starting with a numeral:

UGLY   *35 employees are expected to leave the firm this year.*

BETTER   *This year, 35 employees are expected to leave the firm.*

Use figures to express specific amounts and large numbers:

The authority stated that 21,456 firms were actively operating in the City during December. The hotel was finally sold for £620,000.

Try to be consistent within a sentence:

WRONG   *During the survey the team counted forty-two thrushes, 12 magpies and 15 pied wagtails.*

CORRECT   *During the survey the team counted 42 thrushes, 12 magpies and 15 pied wagtails.*

CORRECT   *The caterer employed 30 women for 3 weeks at £170 a week.*

CORRECT   *The caterer employed thirty women for three weeks at £170 a week.*

Where two numbers adjoin remove the visual confusion by spelling out one and expressing the other in numerals:

CONFUSING   *In 1991 37 people were executed in Djakarta.*

CLEARER   *In 1991, thirty-seven people were executed in Djakarta.*

CONFUSING   *We're selling 4 3-bedroom flats for under £150,000 each.*

CLEARER   *We're selling four 3-bedroom flats for under £150,000 each.*

Expressing Time

Except where the 24-hour clock is required for technical reasons, use the 12-hour clock, indicating morning or afternoon:

> *8.30 am   5.15 pm   11.00 pm   12.00 midnight*
> *8:30 am   5:15 pm   11:00 pm   12:00 midnight*

Of the two styles the single stop separating hours and minutes seems to be preferred, with am and pm expressed without stops. When the time is spelled out, also spell out whether it is morning or afternoon:

> *They arranged to meet at ten in the morning.*
> *We arrived at half-past four in the afternoon.*

Dates

The following styles are generally accepted:

- *Friday, October 29, 1999.* However, many individuals and publishers write the day before the month: Monday, 5 January, 1994 or 12th March, 1986.

- *September 26, 1998*

- *September 1998* (no separating comma)

- *December 17* (preferred); *December 17th; 17 December; 17th December*

- *March 6 - 23, 1998; March 6th - 23rd, 1998*

- *1975-6; 1975-79; 1914-18* but *1975-1985; 1939-1945*

- *1980s; 70s;* but *swinging sixties; gay nineties, roaring twenties*

- *20th century; twentieth century*

- *160BC; AD225*

Ages

As a general rule, numerals convey ages with greater clarity than when spelled out, but either form is acceptable:

- *The wanted man is aged between 50 and 55.*

- *Among the missing is a 7-year-old girl.*

- *They left an 18-month-old child.*

- *Mr Morgan was believed to be in his late eighties* (preferred to *80s*).

Ordinal Numbers

- *first, third, eighth, nineteenth, sixty-fourth* (up to *a hundredth*), then use numerals: *101st, 112th, 143rd,* etc.

- but *a thousandth, millionth.*

- *5th Avenue, 42nd Street, 38th parallel.*

Fractions

- *three-quarters, half-dozen, half-hour, two-thirds* (hyphenated).

- *half a dozen, quarter of an hour, two thirds of the country* (unhyphenated).

Keep numerical expressions consistent; don't mix fractions and percentages in the same sentence:

WRONG   *While almost two out of three were for the recommendations, a worrying 28% voted against them.*

CORRECT   *While just under 65% voted for the recommendations, a worrying 28% voted against them.*

Dimensions and Measurements

Generally, figures are clearer and preferable: *7ft 3in by 5ft 4in; 2.4 by 3.3 metres; 3lbs 12oz; 6.55kg; 6 parts gin, 1 part vermouth; 35ft yacht; 6-inch blade.*

Money

Except for very large amounts *(four billion pound's worth of shares)* and when treated idiomatically *(she looked like a million dollars)* numerals are preferred:

> *£8.99; 49p; £1,000; $5,500; £3.4m; a £6.5bn loan*
> (often spelled out: *'a six-and-a-half billion pound loan'*
> or *'a £6.5 billion loan'* because large amounts are
> difficult to grasp – figuratively and literally).

Put Your Punctuation to the Test!

If a learning curve has its moment of truth, perhaps you've reached that point right now. Dare you put your punctuation skills to the test? You can skip this challenge of course, but on the other hand wouldn't it be smugly reassuring to know that, compared with the majority of English users, you're a polished punctuator? Here's your chance to find out. And if things don't go as well as you hoped . . . it's *your* secret.

Scoring. Points are awarded according to the difficulty of each exercise. Answers to the exercises and scoring guide are on page 171.

---

1.   The Irish humourist J P Donleavy had a singular way with punctuation. The American poet e e cummings eschewed capital letters, even to the extent of spelling his name without them. They collaborated on a joint literary exercise but soon ran into trouble and abandoned the project, preferring the comforts of a nearby bar. Here's what they left us. By any standards it needs repunctuating. At least 40 marks are required to make sense of the piece.

*you wouldnt believe it but there she was sitting at the desk
doing her nail's there was a gun on the desk Miss Marvells
gun I dont know "Miss Marvell that gun there"
"yes
well its a strange thing to be lying on a desk wouldnt you
agree" its just an ordinary gun nothing strange about it
Barnes' didnt know what to say (he hardly ever did – so he
just stood there feeling like a fullblown Johny come lately
"dyou mind if i sit down he asked weakly"
"its a free county" she said.*   **(20)**

2.   Here are some recent newspaper headlines in which the
punctuation is a little awry. Correct each headline for two points
a piece.

A   *PRINCE CHARLES PAL IN M4 CRASH.*   **(2)**

B   *PENSIONS SCANDAL; MANY VICTIM'S STORIES.*   **(2)**

C   *SIX TREATED FOR BEE'S STINGS.*   **(2)**

D   *TODAYS N. IRELAND VOTE RESULTS*   **(2)**

E   *LADIES RUSH TICKETS FOR RACING'S
        LADY'S DAY.*   **(2)**

3.   Are you a hotshot with hyphens? Here are five little teasers
each worth two points if you get them correct:

A   Is it *unself-conscious, unselfconscious,*
        or *un-selfconscious?*   **(2)**

B   Is it a *ten-year-old child*, a *ten-year-old-child*,
        a *ten year old child*, or a *ten-year old child?*   **(2)**

C   Is it an *all star cast*, or an *all-star cast?*   **(2)**

D   Is it: ● *six part- and four full-time employees,*

● *six part and four fulltime employees,*

● *six part-time and four full-time employees*, or

● *six part-time and four fulltime employees*?   **(2)**

E   Is it *fifty odd years* or *fifty-odd years?*   **(2)**

4.   Here's a passage from Jane Austen's novel *Sense and Sensibility*. The original is a single sentence daintily embroidered, in Jane's inimitable style, with no fewer than 13 commas. See if you can pick up Jane's quill and reinstate them in their proper places. If you replace all of them correctly you earn 10 points. For every one you miss or misplace, delete a point.

> *In her earnest meditations on the contents of the letter on the depravity of that mind which could dictate it and probably on the very different mind of a very different person who had no other connection whatever with the affair than what her heart gave him with everything that passed Elinor forgot the immediate distress of her sister forgot that she had three letters on her lap yet unread and so entirely forgot how long she had been in the room that when on hearing a carriage drive up to the door she went to the window to see who could be coming so unreasonably early she was all astonishment to perceive Mrs Jennings's chariot which she knew had not been ordered till one.*   **(10)**

5.   Here are five short exercises involving direct speech and quotation. Each is worth three points if you get all the punctuation and quotation marks in the right places.

A *Did anyone call while I was out Jamie's mother asked.* **(3)**

B *Will you, Fred asked for the third time, pass me that plate.* **(3)**

C *Mr Hayward said that George's pay would be £240 a week.* **(3)**

D *Please come immediately the message said.* **(3)**

E *Descartes didn't actually say I think, therefore I am, but Cogito, ergo sum.* **(3)**

6. Here the writer is having trouble with his parenthesising. It's worth five points if you can make the necessary corrections.

> *We decided to explore the High Street, (in York) but soon discovered that it meandered, lost its way, traversed a couple of squares (at one stage Fiona asked, "are they really serious?" but did, in the end take us to the other side of the city.* **(5)**

7. Lastly, here's a mixed bag of marks. Of the following 15 examples, some are correct in terms of punctuation and some are not. Your task is to determine which ones are correct. Mark with a tick or cross as you go and score 2 points for each success.

a. *Are the philosophers invariably right? asks Jeremy Hardy.*

b. *Her exam subjects include mathematics, English, Chemistry, Latin, geography and theatre studies.*

c. *Ones inclination is to avoid one's worst prejudices.*

d. *Will Mr and Mrs Jacobs be accompanying us next Tuesday?*

e. *MINISTER APPRISED OF ART GALLERIES PROBLEMS.*

f.   *Walter bought a forty gallon water butt for the garden.*

g.   *20% off Ski's and Clothing this month only.*

h.   *We were all hoping for an Indian Summer.*

i.   *They spent the weekend in what was described as an "alcoholic haze".*

j.   *The stall was selling bargain T-shirt's and girls' frocks.*

k.   *The neighbours lived by taking in one another's washing.*

l.   *The experience was for him, as for her, quite devastating.*

m.   *James took the car, the tank was almost empty.*

n.   *The cop looked at him; filthy, bloodied, drunk – and fighting mad.*

o.   *The upholsterer did a great job recovering the settee.*   **(30)**

Answers and Scoresheet

1.   Between them Donleavy and cummings made a hash of their punctuation. Here's the way a normal user of the English language would express the passage:

> *You wouldn't believe it, but there she was, sitting at the desk doing her nails. There was a gun on the desk. Miss Marvell's gun? I don't know.*
> *"Miss Marvell – that gun there – "*
> *"Yes?"*
> *"Well, it's a strange thing to be lying on a desk, wouldn't you agree?"*
> *"It's just an ordinary gun. Nothing strange about it."*

*Barnes didn't know what to say (he hardly ever did), so he
just stood there feeling like a full-blown Johnny-come-lately.
"D'you mind if I sit down?" he asked weakly.
"It's a free country," she said.*

Scoring. Altogether there are no less than 45 punctuation
errors, omissions or redundant marks. If you identified 40 or more,
award yourself the full 20 points. But if you didn't, for every error
you failed to find, deduct a point. For example, if you found only
32 mistakes, deduct 8 points, so that your score for the exercise is
20 - 8 = 12. If you identified only 25 mistakes, deduct 15 points:
20 - 15 = 5.

Your score:

2. Here are the headlines, this time with correct punctuation:

A *PRINCE CHARLES'S PAL IN M4 CRASH.*
or *PRINCE CHARLES' PAL IN M4 CRASH.* **2 points**

B *PENSIONS SCANDAL VICTIMS' STORIES.*
The pensions scandal resulted in many victims
(plural), and many victims' (plural possessive
apostrophe) stories. **2 points**

C *SIX TREATED FOR BEE STINGS.*
As it was, the headline inferred that one bee
was responsible for all six stings. But a bee can
only sting once. It would be correct to say,
SIX TREATED FOR BEES' STINGS but using the
adjective/plural noun combination is simpler. **2 points**

D *TODAY'S N. IRELAND VOTE RESULTS* **2 points**

E   *LADIES RUSH TICKETS FOR RACING'S LADIES' DAY.*
The Ladies' Day is obviously meant for more
than one lady, hence the plural possessive
apostrophe.   **2 points**

                                    Your score:

3.   You shouldn't have had a hang-up (the noun is hyphenated;
hang up is the verb) about the five hyphenating exercises:

A   *unselfconscious* (no hyphen)   **2 points**

B   *ten-year-old child*   **2 points**

C   *all-star cast*   **2 points**

D   *six part-time and four full-time employees* is
the wholly correct version which has both
part-time and *full-time* consistent with hyphens.
However the version *six part- and four full-time
employees* is also correct although a little clumsy
with its suspensive or 'hanging' hyphen.   **2 points**

E   *fifty-odd years.* Without the hyphen those
fifty years would have been very odd indeed!   **2 points**

                                    Your score:

4.   Here is Jane Austen's original, with all the commas reinstated:

*In her earnest meditations on the contents of the letter, on the
depravity of that mind which could dictate it, and, probably,
on the very different mind of a very different person, who had
no other connection whatever with the affair than what her
heart gave him with everything that passed, Elinor forgot the*

> *immediate distress of her sister, forgot that she had three
> letters on her lap yet unread, and so entirely forgot how long
> she had been in the room, that when, on hearing a carriage
> drive up to the door, she went to the window to see who could
> be coming so unreasonably early, she was all astonishment to
> perceive Mrs Jennings's chariot, which she knew had not
> been ordered till one.*

If you correctly reinstated all 13 commas, award yourself a well-deserved 10 points, for imitating Jane's attenuated sentences is far from easy. But for every comma not replaced, or placed in the wrong position, deduct a point. If, for example, you managed to replace only seven of the commas correctly, deduct 6 points, giving you a score of 10-6 = 4.

Your score: ☐

5.   Check the solutions closely to see if you have all your quotation marks and other punctuation correct:

A   *'Did anyone call while I was out?' Jamie's
mother asked.*

Note that the direct question requires a question
mark inside the closing quotation mark.   **3 points**

B   *'Will you,' Fred asked for the third time,
'pass me that plate.'*

A question mark after *plate* is optional, as at
his third attempt Fred is requesting rather
than merely asking a question.   **3 points**

C   *Mr Hayward said that George's pay would be
£240 a week.*

	The sentence is entirely correct.	**3 points**
D	*'Please come immediately,' the message said.*	**3 points**
E	*Descartes didn't exactly say, 'I think, therefore I am', but, 'Cogito, ergo sum'.*	
	A version without commas after *say* and *but* would be considered correct, but note that the comma after *am* and the stop after *sum* are outside the closing quotation marks.	**3 points**

Your score: [ ]

6. Here's the correctly parenthesised passage:

> *We decided to explore the High Street (in York), but soon discovered that it meandered, lost its way, traversed a couple of squares (at one stage Fiona asked, "are they really serious?") but did, in the end, take us to the other side of the city.*

There were three errors: (1) comma comes *after* the parenthesised *(in York)*, not before; (2) the parenthesis begun before *at one stage* was not completed after *serious*, and likewise (3) the parenthetical phrase *in the end* was not enclosed by a *pair* of commas. If you spotted and corrected all three errors, award yourself the full five points, but deduct two points for each one you missed.

Your score: [ ]

7. Of the 15 statements, only four are correct and if you didn't interfere with these they're worth two points each. The remainder all contain errors. If you spotted these and made the corrections they're also worth two points apiece:

a. *Are the philosophers invariably right, asks Jeremy Hardy.* (no question mark)

b. *Her exam subjects include mathematics, English, chemistry, Latin, geography and theatre studies.* (no capital for chemistry)

c. *One's inclination is to avoid one's worst prejudices.* (possessive apostrophe required for one's inclination)

d. *Will Mr and Mrs Jacobs be accompanying us next Tuesday?* (correct)

e. *MINISTER APPRISED OF ART GALLERIES' PROBLEMS.* (possessive apostrophe required for *GALLERIES' PROBLEMS*)

f. *Walter bought a forty-gallon water butt for the garden.* (*forty-gallon* is hyphenated)

g. *20% off Skis and Clothing this month only* (apostrophe in *Skis* redundant)

h. *We were all hoping for an indian summer.* (no capitals for *indian summer*)

i. *They spent the weekend in what was described as an "alcoholic haze".* (correct)

j. *The stall was selling bargain T-shirts and girls' frocks.* (no apostrophe required in T-shirts)

k.   *The neighbours lived by taking in one another's washing.*
     (correct)

l.   *The experience was for him, as for her, quite devastating.*
     (correct)

m.   *James took the car; the tank was almost empty.*

     (The 'comma splice' won't make these two thoughts
     into a single sentence. A colon or semicolon would be
     acceptable, and so would two separate sentences:
     James took the car. The tank was almost empty.)

n.   *The cop looked at him: filthy, bloodied, drunk – and fighting
     mad.* (a colon, not a semicolon, required after him)

o.   *The upholsterer did a great job re-covering the settee.*
     (Unless the upholsterer was recovering the settee for
     non-payment, a hyphen is required to make clear that
     he had given the settee a new cover).

Your score:

Well? If you scored the full 100 points you are, without a
doubt, a punctuation prodigy – congratulations! Any score above
90 entitles you to consider yourself a very polished punctuator, and
if you managed 80 points you are certainly proficient.

When this quiz was originally road-tested among several
groups of teenagers and adults representing a wide range of
writing and communication skills, the average score was 56 points.
Feel better?

Index

Collins Wordpower

English is the most widely used language in the world, yet it is also one of the easiest languages to be misunderstood in. The Collins Wordpower series is the ultimate in user-friendliness for all who have wished for an authoritative, comprehensive yet accessible range of guides through the maze of English usage. Designed for ease of use and illustrated by top cartoonists, these books will enrich your powers of communication – whether in speech, writing, comprehension or general knowledge – and they are fun to use!

PUNCTUATION
0 00 472373 2
How to handle the 'nuts and bolts' of English prose £5.99

GOOD GRAMMAR
0 00 472374 0
How to break down the barriers between you and clear communication £5.99

SUPER SPELLER
0 00 472371 6
How to master the most difficult-to-spell words and names in the English language £5.99

GOOD WRITING
0 00 472381 3
How to write clear and grammatically correct English £5.99

VOCABULARY EXPANDER
0 00 472382 1
How to dramatically increase your word power £5.99

ABBREVIATIONS
0 00 472389 9
The complete guide to abbreviations and acronyms £5.99

FOREIGN PHRASES
0 00 472388 0
The most commonly used foreign words in the English language £5.99

WORD CHECK
0 00 472378 3
How to deal with difficult and confusable words £5.99